PRAY FOR SEEDS

Pray for Seeds

Leadership That Generates Spiritual Life and Growth

PAUL T. HOBBS
DESMOND BARRETT

Foreword by Shawn Siegfreid

WIPF & STOCK • Eugene, Oregon

PRAY FOR SEEDS
Leadership That Generates Spiritual Life and Growth

Wipf & Stock
An Imprint of Wipf and Stock Publishers
199 W. 8th Ave., Suite 3
Eugene, OR 97401

www.wipfandstock.com

PAPERBACK ISBN: 979-8-3852-7126-9
HARDCOVER ISBN: 979-8-3852-7127-6
EBOOK ISBN: 979-8-3852-7128-3

VERSION NUMBER 04/01/26

Contents

Foreword

It is both an honor and a privilege to write the foreword for my friends and Colleagues, Dr. Paul Hobbs, and Dr. Desmond Barrett. We have the joy of serving together in the Church of the Nazarene. During my past eighteen months as district superintendent, I have come to know them as thoughtful pastors, trusted leaders, and, as this book clearly demonstrates, gifted authors.

In *Pray for Seeds: Leadership That Generates Spiritual Life and Growth*, Dr. Hobbs and Dr. Barrett draw from a rich blend of academic insight and lived pastoral experience. As academics and practitioners, they bring wisdom that is deeply rooted in Scripture while remaining keenly aware of the realities facing the church in today's post-Christian context. This is not theory for theory's sake; it is guidance forged in classrooms, churches, and communities where real leaders are laboring faithfully.

I found myself repeatedly underlining and highlighting passages throughout this book—insights that spoke directly to my own calling as I walk alongside pastors and congregations seeking spiritual vitality and meaningful growth. The authors have a way of naming our challenges honestly while never surrendering hope. Their vision for leadership is both realistic and faith-filled, calling leaders and laypeople alike to cultivate environments where spiritual life can take root and flourish.

I enthusiastically recommend *Pray for Seeds* to our denomination and, indeed, to the wider church. Paul and Desmond close this book on a hopeful and compelling note, reminding us that the church's best days can still lie ahead. As we pray for seed and faithfully tend the soil God has entrusted to us, this book will serve as a timely and encouraging companion in the work of growing Christ's church.

REV. SHAWN SIEGFREID
District Superintendent of the Southern California District of the Church of the Nazarene

1

The Generation and Transfer of Life and Growth

Living near a place locally famous for its apple orchards has its perks. Its popularity makes it a little difficult to go through town in September, but I can ride my mountain bike up and over some oak-tree-filled hills to enjoy all things apples. The ride burns enough calories that I can indulge in apple donuts, pie, cider, and even a fried apple burrito. On good days, I just stick to an apple right off the tree and head on home. This wonderful place is called Oak Glenn and it is situated in the foothills of the San Bernardino Mountains in Southern California. Not only is it a great place for apples, but it is also where I spend time enjoying a beautiful place to pray.

Praying in a place filled with apples reminded me of an old leadership saying that I first heard while in Bible college thirty years ago. My professors had years of experience so the saying is probably older than I am. One of the versions of the saying is, "Turn your apple cart too fast and you will lose all the apples." My professor was teaching on the topic of organizational change and making the point that if we made changes in our churches too fast, we would risk losing a large portion of the congregation. Because most of us soon-to-be pastors, would begin our ministries pastoring very small congregations, losing people would most likely end with a church closure. Therefore, I took this saying to heart and committed to applying it to my pastoral leadership.

Upon graduation, I held up my commitment and lead my first congregation by instituting slow collaborative change. It worked well and those serving alongside me appreciated the opportunity to be part of a team instead of just being told what to do. Whenever we had major decisions to make, we committed to a month of prayer that included weekly fasting. Through these periods of prayer, God was faithful and unified our leadership. Leaders unified through prayer creates teams capable of initiating and instituting lasting, effective change. Serving with those leaders shaped my leadership as I would go on to plant a church and almost a decade later move into a revitalization appointment.

Being in the revitalization appointment, I had to speed up the change process because this church was on the verge of closing. The denominational leader overseeing the church called and said that he was going to close the church or send me if I was willing. When I accepted the position, I knew that slow change was not an option. Thankfully, the few remaining members agreed with the denominational leader that change had to be immediate. When I arrived, I met some wonderful people who were open to praying and seeking God for new direction. The only thing they requested was that I allowed their weekly potluck meal to continue. I like food, so I was on board with leaving that alone. Every once in a while, that meal includes an apple pie from Oak Glenn.

My first few years in this setting were, as you can imagine, both exciting and frustrating. Through the immediate changes, God reset the direction of the church and we were moving forward. No, we did not become a megachurch, or even a large church. However, church members began to experience new life in themselves because they were aligning their prayer life with biblical principles. If you desire the same, keep reading. *Praying for Seeds* is not a church growth strategy or evangelism tool for church leaders. Our goal is to help every leader align their prayer life with biblical principles of sowing and reaping. As we do, we will reap a harvest of righteousness.

Personally, aligning my prayer life with the biblical principles discussed in this book became evident as I reevaluated the old saying of turning the apple cart too fast. As I prayed about my response to what God was doing in my personal life and the church, the old saying was brought to mind, but with a twist. The twist came from the words of a friend who stated, "It's not how many apples are in the cart, but how many seeds in the apples." As I pondered this concept I thought about the people in my church. Did they have any seeds? Did I? In other words, were we experiencing a harvest of righteousness? Did we have the capacity to produce fruit, leading others to become followers of Jesus? Honestly, I was unsure. I doubted that the people making up the congregation I served had any interest in helping others come to faith in Jesus and if I was in error as their pastor. I wondered if we were seedless apples.

Pondering this reality was not comfortable because I love those I lead. They support and respect me beyond what I deserve and they are great people. They serve when no one else will and show tremendous dedication to each other, but we were not seeing many people come to Jesus. I doubted them and myself. To gain a biblical perspective, I needed a better understanding of the seed analogy. Therefore, I did what we all do: I grabbed my concordance and read all the Scriptures that contained the words "seed" and "seeds." I also read the related passages about sowing and harvesting. What I discovered changed the way I pray for myself, my family, and each member of our church. It also shaped my understanding of how God works through his people. I began to see that seeds generate and transfer life and growth.

With a new understanding of the purpose of seed, I sought to comprehend the various types of seed in the Bible. My question became, what exactly does God use to generate and transfer life and growth? I knew that it could not be the things that I was focusing on as church leader and child of God. I was stressed and losing focus. My concerns were our church's marketability, online presence, a properly maintained image, and my own success. The things left me feeling discouraged and seedless. I had to regain my focus and get my spiritual life back in line with who God created me to be, so I set out to recalibrate my heart to the Scripture and asked my coauthor to join in the journey.

Our study on the topic of seeds led to identifying six seeds. Studying these passages brought heavy conviction and opened my heart to the reality of my poor prayer life. I realized that I was not praying, but complaining and panicking. Throughout this book, Dr. Desmond Barrett and I will discuss what we have learned, with the goal of helping you discover a path to prayer alignment. If you encounter times of conviction, do not give up. Commit to pressing forward into a new season of healthy prayer.

THOUGH US, GOD WILL GENERATE AND TRANSFER LIFE AND GROWTH

Galatians 6:7–10

7 Do not be deceived: God is not mocked, for whatever one sows, that
will he also reap. 8 For the one who sows to his own flesh will from the
flesh reap corruption, but the one who sows to the Spirit will from the
Spirit reap eternal life. 9 And let us not grow weary of doing good, for
in due season we will reap, if we do not give up. 10 So then, as we have
opportunity, let us do good to everyone, and especially to those who
are of the household of faith.

In the following chapters, we will address six types of seeds God uses to transfer life and growth in and through his people. Before looking at each of the six seeds, let's consider the nature and purpose of seed in general from the perspectives of both the Old and New Testaments. Throughout both Testaments, seed is used figuratively to illustrate the generation and transfer of life and growth. This general concept is foundational to understanding how God works in his people. Without this understanding, we will fall into the mistake of believing the six types of seed form a to-do list for blessing, which we all know will produce an insecure relationship with God.

In the Old Testament, seed was seen as God's provision. They understood that God provided seed to produce food (Gen 1:29; 42:1–2; Eccl 11:6). In turn the people would use seed as an offering unto the Lord displaying their trust and reliance in him for their well-being (Lev 23:15–21; 2 Chr 31:5). Because seed held such a place in humanity's relationship with God, it was also used to measure value (Lev 27:16). Once seed was used to measure value, people recognized that its presence was a blessing (Ps 67:6) and its absence a curse (Joel 1:16–17). Humanity's dependence on God for our existence is made obvious within the agricultural setting of the Old Testament.

The dependence of humanity on God then played out in the various regulations of stewardship and appreciation. Seed was not to be mixed when planting a vineyard (Deut 22:9) or watered with water contaminated with an animal carcass (Lev 11:37–38). As these and other restrictions were followed, the seed was held in high regard and was understood to be the source of life. Thus, God was worshiped through the giving of a tithe of the seed (Lev 27:30). These regulations were put in place for these reasons, but they were also creating a mindset of honoring seed that would later be used by Jesus and the writers of the New Testament

In the New Testament, the word "seed" is used figuratively. These uses of "seed" will be explored throughout this book. For now, it is appropriate to note that "seed" is used to illustrate many of the teachings of Jesus, such as the size of our faith (Matt 17), the growth of the kingdom of God (Matt 13:31–32; Mark 4:26–29), and the principle of life from death (John 12:23–25). Other Gospel writers used "seed" figuratively to address matters of discipleship, such as our birth into eternal life (1 John 3:9) and our relationship to the word of God (1 Pet 1:22–25). These figurative uses of "seed" and the concepts of sowing and reaping are based on premises established in the Old Testament. Throughout our lives following Jesus, praying for the seed must be understood and applied with both Testaments in mind. Doing so will open our hearts to the transforming work of God as he generates and transfers life and growth.

LIFE AND GROWTH ARE TRANSFERRED THROUGH SOWING AND REAPING

Galatians 6:7

Do not be deceived: God is not mocked, for whatever one sows, that will he also reap.

This general principle is seen in many places throughout the Bible. One such place is Gal 6:7–10. This passage gives us the framework for properly understanding what is taking place in our spiritual journey. We would do well to place each of the six seeds addressed in this book in the context of what we learn in this text. The concept of sowing and reaping form the proper means to apply everything we will explore together in the coming pages.

The first few words of the text set the tone. We are immediately warned not to be deceived. Living in deception, believing that we are in line with truth when in fact we are not, leads to devastating consequences. Look at what frustrates you about your relationship with Jesus. It probably comes from the seed sown and allowed to germinate in your heart that is leading to deception. If you are reaping anything but righteousness, you are sowing the wrong seed. If so, plow the landscape of your life and plant good seed that will produce what God intends. Pay close attention to what you sow into your heart, for we are easily deceived.

Reflecting on this reality may cause some major regret. Don't be too hard on yourself. Shame has no place in the Christian heart. Godly conviction that calls you to repentance and elevates your sense of worth is part of the journey towards holiness. Shame that devalues you is never part of God's work of identifying sin in your life. Your value is based on the fact that you are created in the image of God and therefore worthy of redemption and restoration. If

God is identifying bad seed, confess it as sin and repent. Be convinced of his great love for you leading to a harvest of righteousness, experienced in each area of your life.

MOTIVE OF SOWING

Galatians 6:8

For the one who sows to his own flesh will from the flesh reap corruption, but the one who sows to the Spirit will from the Spirit reap eternal life.

Being aware of our own heart's openness to deception requires that we pay close attention to our motives and expectations. The text is clear that being motivated by our natural inclinations will lead to corruption. If you have ever been fooled by your own desires, you understand the warning Paul gave the Galatians. You also understand the danger of listening to the current cultural voice, calling us to find fulfillment through self-actualization. The reality of this warning and the ignoring of it is evident within the social ills of our day.

A deceived heart is not always identified by issues typically defined as sin. In my case, wanting to see more people come to know and follow Jesus though the local church is usually seen as a worthy goal. However, this stated desire among pastors and church leaders is all too often clouded by selfishness or insecurity. As those in other occupations, pastors want to feel successful among their peers. We gather at conventions and assemblies, submit statistical reports to denominational leaders and church boards, all under pressure to succeed. It is often concluded that a fruitful pastor has an ever-increasing number of apples in their cart. If we are not keenly aware of our heart's ability to be deceived, we may end up preaching the gospel for selfish gain and thus reaping a harvest of corruption.

A simple but profound question can be addressed to inspect our heart's motivation. What are you expecting to reap by following of Jesus? Make a list of these expectations and compare them to how Jesus describes those who follow him. Are your expectations in line with and based on what Jesus himself states? This helpful exercise may uncover a startling revelation. God may reveal that your heart has been deceived by bad theology based on wish fulfillment, not Scripture. I must consistently ask myself this question when the outcome of my efforts birth frustration and fear. Returning to the biblical record reminds me that what I am experiencing is to be expected. The honesty of the biblical writers helps me navigate and shift my own expectations and put me back in line with following Jesus.

If you are a pastor or a church leader, read what ministry was like in the early church. Yes, there were miracles and seasons of amazing growth. However, there were also times of persecution, rejection, abandonment, imprisonment, and martyrdom. We should expect both today and not be surprised if the best moments are within the context of the most unexpected circumstances. We cannot be motivated by the bright lights of the platform while forgetting about the dark nights of the soul. Surround yourself with other leaders who will care less about your success and more about the harvest of righteousness within your own heart and home.

LIFE AND GROWTH ARE TRANSFERRED IN DUE SEASON

GALATIANS 6:9

And let us not grow weary of doing good, for in due season we will reap, if we do not give up.

Once properly motivated, the waiting begins. Notice the phrase "in due season," which may torment impatient leaders finding themselves under the pressure of required change. Leaders often believe there is no time for waiting, but wait they must. Patience is an important step toward meaningful and lasting change. Remember the previously mentioned adage of turning the cart too quickly? Forgetting it can cause us to lose patients and derail our otherwise properly motivated progress.

Admittedly, waiting often feels like wasting. However, refuse to fall into this misguided mindset. Waiting for the "due season" is filled with "doing good," not just sitting around turning the pages of our calendars or filling them with unproductive trivialities. Keep doing the good that moves the mission forward, knowing full well that you may not see the fruit of your labors for a long time. Experienced leaders are no strangers to this and have developed leadership persistence that help their followers and co-laborers stay the course. The natural human response to prolonged laborious waiting is to grow weary and give up. Now may not be the season of reaping, but we will never reap if we don't wait.

To push past the natural human response of growing weary in the waiting, we must remember that our work is not in vain. Every aspect of Christian leadership is contextualized in the work of Jesus. In his first advent, Jesus became the firstfruit of the resurrection, and at his return, he will complete the harvest and destroy every other power and authority (1 Cor 15:23–24). Today, we are somewhere in the process of what he has accomplished and that which remains. We have been called to lead within this context; therefore our weariness can be overcome by the knowledge that our labor is not in vain (1 Cor 15:58) and will be completed at the return of Christ.

This big picture is the motivation that will move you forward. It is bigger than every challenge you face as a leader. Refuse to be weighed down by the nagging daily pressures of leadership. We all understand the realty that doing ministry today requires resources of time, talents, and treasures. God will provide what is necessary for you to fulfill your calling. Keep doing good with who and what he supplies. What good can you do today with what you have now that will produce fruit in the future? In other words, plant what little seed you have.

TAKE EVERY OPPORTUNITY TO TRANSFER LIFE AND GROWTH

GALATIANS 6:10

So then, as we have opportunity, let us do good to everyone, and especially to those who are of the household of faith.

Every leader can easily miss these opportunities, and of course no one will see them all even at our best. On days when we are not our best, we can be blinded by the busyness of our ministries as we attempt to fulfill everything in our job descriptions. Busy blindness can make opportunities seem like distractions. Do we ever read of Jesus frustratingly viewing people as distractions? Of course not, but if you lived with me, you would hear me say to myself, "I don't have time for that person right now." This is not to say that we should be on call 24/7, but it does mean that we should create enough margin in our schedules that allows us to serve others as we have opportunity. We are going to miss some, and will never get this perfect, but there may be room for significant growth.

Growing in our ability to maximize opportunities to do good requires that we understand what is truly in our power. Proverbs 3:27 is helpful, revealing, "Do not withhold good from those it is due, when it is in your power to do it." This is an amazing reality that helps us understand how to navigate our opportunities. It helps by posing a couple questions. First, is the person due the good in question? Secondly, is it within my power to do something? If the answer to both questions are "yes," then we should help. If one of those questions is "no," it may be best for us to say, "Withhold help." Be very careful not to use these two questions as excuses to avoid uncomfortable situations, but use honest, prayer-inspired discernment. Remember, we are looking for growth, not perfection.

The last part of the verse under consideration helps us further navigate how we are to transfer life and growth through taking opportunity to do good. Paul tells the Galatian church to give priority to those in the household of faith. This may seem counterintuitive for many leaders who have the gift of evangelism or structure their ministries with a compassionate focus. However, this inspired, authoritative statement can be a compassionately evangelic display of the care God's people show to one another. We must begin within the family. With this starting point, and the discernment of the proverb mentioned above, we can begin to create an understanding of what God requires of us in this vital area of leadership.

I believe this will include at least two very important truths. Remember that God does not violate his laws or principles. The law of sowing and reaping is one of them. We are taught in 2 Cor 9:6–10 that "whoever sows sparingly will also reap sparingly, and whoever sows bountifully will also reap bountifully." Additionally, this same text reveals, "*He who supplies seed to the sower and bread for food will supply and multiply your seed for sowing and increase the harvest of your righteousness*" (emphasis added). This helps us understand that we can only give to others what God has given us. May you sow abundantly as you have opportunity.

CONCLUDING PRAYER CHALLENGE

I stated earlier that I live in a beautiful place to pray. You probably do as well, and I invite you to step out into that space for a time of prayer before reading any further. Preferably, that place will allow you to experience the beauty of God. In this time of prayer, I encourage you to ask God the serious question: Lord, in what ways are my prayers out of line with your word and the calling you have placed on my life? I am asking God to reveal his answer to each reader of this book. The revelation you receive can serve as a guide for the remaining chapters. As you venture out, take an apple or two. They can remind you that what you are enjoying is the result of a seed that is now generating and transferring life and growth.

2

Seeds That Produce a Harvest of Righteousness

Admittedly, my heart is not always in the right place or fully prepared for the work of God. Worship gatherings and board meetings are two environments that become toxic when a leader's heart is misaligned with God's intended purpose. When structuring weekly and monthly routines, I create a margin around these events for the purpose of heart reorientation. This includes setting aside my phone after 6:00 p.m. on Saturday evenings and prolonged physical exercise prior to board meetings. The benefits of unplugging and physical activity help clear my mind and heart so that I can be fully present before the Lord as I lead.

These two activities may not sound pastoral or spiritual so let me explain. I used to prepare for these events with additional reading, listening to messages from other pastors, and worship music. These were not helpful. They only consumed me, filling my mind with further thinking about the content of the worship service and the board meeting agenda. They did not help my heart. To be fully present at both, I need to totally disengage to reengage. Church leaders are an odd bunch. Consumed with all things church-related, we forget how to think and feel like a child of God. Forgetting this can corrupt our hearts, sending us to dangerous emotional and spiritual places. Maybe a psychiatrist can explain this more clearly, but I am better when I do these two things. In case you are wondering, yes, I read Scripture and pray every day.

As you read this chapter, listen very closely to what God reveals to you about your heart at this stage in your leadership experience. New leaders, it's a good time to check your motives. The work that is before you is not easy. You will not lead long if your heart is not well prepared at the outset. Experienced leaders, are you currently sensing the joy of obedience, knowing that you are in the middle of his will and fully committed to the call God placed on your heart years ago? What course redirection is necessary? Leaders approaching retirement, is your heart prepared to finish well? At each stage of leadership, like soil is prepared for seed, our hearts need preparation for the work God desires to do in and through us.

In this chapter, I will discuss two important ways to prepare your heart through repentance. This helps realign our hearts toward God, creating good soil for life-producing seed. You will be challenged to fall at his feet in full transparency, knowing that his call is upon your life and you belong to him. Your leadership journey is not complete, and he has much more to do through you for the sake of others. This work was borne in his heart and placed within you by the Holy Spirit. Refuse to surrender to anything but him. Set aside your expectations of what the ministry should look like. Let go of comparing your journey to the pastors around you. Lean in to God's will and he will guide you forward beginning with the creation of a righteous heart.

A RIGHTEOUS HEART IS THE SOIL FOR SEED

Like soil is prepared for seed, our heart needs to be prepared for the work God wants to do in and through us. This is one reason why I believe in a rigorous ministry preparation process. Understanding that many called into ministry are not in the position to earn a college degree, denominations often offer educational processes that prepare those called to serve. Either way, do not skip the process. You may have extensive ministry experience prior to a call to lead, but that experience is not a replacement for proper training. Refuse to undervalue the academic experience, but see it as a significant means of heart preparation.

When I entered my ministry preparation in the early 1990s, God revealed a reality that all these years later continues to shape my heart. As I entered the classroom at Nazarene Bible College for the first time, the professor had a descriptive list of pastoral attributes written on the whiteboard. As I took my seat, I was overwhelmed. Some weeks later as I thought about my less than perfect GPA, God reminded me of that list and spoke to my heart. He taught me that I was not learning how to do something; I was becoming someone. His Spirit was shaping me into a person that he could use to further his mission in the world. The first step in this process was repentance.

REPENTANCE PREPARES OUR HEART FOR GOD'S BLESSING

Jeremiah 4:1–4

1 "If you return, O Israel, declares the LORD, to me you should return.
If you remove your detestable things from my presence, and do not
waver, 2 and if you swear, 'As the LORD lives,' in truth, in justice, and
in righteousness, then nations shall bless themselves in him, and in
him shall they glory." 3 For thus says the LORD to the men of Judah and
Jerusalem: "Break up your fallow ground, and sow not among thorns.
4 Circumcise yourselves to the LORD; remove the foreskin of your
hearts, O men of Judah and inhabitants of Jerusalem; lest my wrath go
forth like fire, and burn with none to quench it, because of the evil of
your deeds."

The first word of this passage, as translated in the English Standard Version, is "if." This word makes the blessings included conditional. Though it is not a popular thought, many of God's blessings are conditional. I would go so far as to say that our calling to serve as ministry leaders is a conditional blessing. We cannot allow detestable things to remain in our heart and expect our work and life to be blessed. God's glory cannot be seen though the corrupted heart of a leader. As a leader, keep open accounts with the Lord by quick repentance and a heart receptive of his corrective hand.

In this text, God specifically identifies two key issues. The first is detestable things in his presence. The second was the Israelites' propensity to waver. Compare this to the overly relaxed misuse of God's grace in today's church, along with what many have called the Great Resignation. As church leaders, we have the propensity to set up our own idols and self-promotion and worldly success. When we suffer because of them, we waver in our commitment to fulfill our call to ministry. Repenting of this common condition opens and heals our hearts, preparing us for a revival of God's Spirit. If you are wavering, seek revival sparked by personal repentance.

Sparked by repentance, this personal revival is a commitment to be blessed and glory in him as he lives in truth, justice, and righteousness. Israel was supposed to live and lead with a commitment to these three aspects of God's ever-present nature. However, it was never enough for them. They consistently attempted to add the gods of surrounding nations because they were not satisfied with God alone. Pastors and church leaders are susceptible to this same failure and it's a pressing problem for me personally. I want God and significance. How about you? Do you have a "God and" mentality? I have been fighting mine for years and pray just about every Sunday that God would help me be satisfied with him alone. It's a constant battle and I feel like I am calling out in repentance all the time. I am praying that God creates in me an appreciative heart, satisfied with being in the center of his will. I want to serve well and rest in the knowledge of pleasing him. This is the blessing I seek.

REPENTANCE PREPARES THE HEART FOR GOD'S RIGHTEOUSNESS

Hosea 10:12

Sow for yourselves righteousness; reap steadfast love; break up your fallow ground, for it is the time to seek the LORD, that he may come and rain righteousness upon you.

The many successes of the Israelites often did not result in worshiping the One True God. Instead, they worshiped foreign gods and failed to be the people and blessing God intended. Over and over again, the people of God did not act according to their identity and purpose. They allowed themselves to be swept up into the popular current of their day. Like many of us, they believed or at least behaved as though punishment and discipline did not exist. They abused and took for granted the grace of God. Although Hosea, living in the final days of the Northern Kingdom, was used by God to name the army that would be raised for the purposes of punishment, he also spoke of the promise of restoration. In the preexilic prophets, you will notice the pattern of warning, punishment, and promise of restoration. Perhaps we should repent in seasons of warning.

Though the warned did not escape punishment, God remained faithful. Restoration would come through repentance and God would once again "rain righteousness" on his people. Verse 12 is a call to repentance and the revelation of the promised restoration. This was not an isolated text or a one-time promise to a select number of people. It is a revelation of how God works. My fellow leader, if you find yourself in a season of fruitless ministry and personal hardship, I encourage you to think and pray deeply about this reality. Begin again to "sow for yourself righteousness" so that you can "reap steadfast love." In the previous chapter I discussed that God will not violate his principle of sowing and reaping. Perhaps your fruitless season is the result of disobedience and ungodly sowing. If so, restoration and revitalization may only be a prayer of repentance away. God can once again qualify you for fruitful ministry.

Hosea further commands the people of the Northern Kingdom to "break up your fallow ground." Has your heart become hardened by the stress of ministry? Have you been swept away by the current of our cultural context? Perhaps you have been experiencing what many define as success and yet you feel like the fruit is rotting on the vine. The bigger your ministry becomes, the more lost and out of control you feel. It is time to seek the Lord, beginning with softening your heart towards him. Refrain from praying demanding prayers and rest in the provision of his Spirit. Give back to him that you have taken for yourself. Remember that repentance prepares your heart to receive from God. As you submit yourself to him in humble repentance, your heart will once again be the soil in which God sows his righteousness. The fruit of ministry will not rot on the vine and become a stench. It will again be the overflow of your personal devotion to him instead of your allegiance to others whose applause we often seek.

As our fallow ground is broken and God rains down his righteousness in your hearts, we will be able to sow righteousness in the lives of others. Proverbs 11:18 states, "The wicked earns deceptive wages, but one who sows righteousness gets a sure reward." The next verse suggests that the reward may be life. Verse 19 states, "Whoever is steadfast in righteousness will live, but he who pursues evil will die." The value is sowing righteousness because in so doing life is being produced.

Think about how much effort is wasted because it fails to produce life and growth. Many things that leaders do fit into the category of wasted energy. Self-promotion may be at the top of the list. Everyday leaders waste time and energy in self-promotion masked as service unto God. Posting pictures of the poor receiving help from your congregation may look praiseworthy, but it could also be humiliating for those coming to your church for help. Before clicking "Post" or "Share," think about what you are sowing. Righteous praise to the Lord, or shameless self-promotion? Only pour out what he pours in. Make sowing righteousness your aim and you will dwell in a fruitful field as portrayed by the prophet Elijah: "Then justice will dwell in the wilderness, and righteousness abide in the fruitful field" (Isa 32:16).

FULFILL YOUR MINISTRY IN PEACE AND JUSTICE BY SOWING SEEDS OF RIGHTEOUSNESS

Upon repentance, God blesses and works his righteousness in us resulting in peace. His seed of righteousness often operates on the unseen level. Don't think about programming or style but think about your heart's motive. As we have been discussing, righteousness is God's work in his people, and it begins in the heart of the leader. With God's righteousness shaping your heart, you can sow seeds of peace. In the third chapter of his epistle, James writes, "And a harvest of righteousness is sown in peace by those who make peace" (Jas 3:18). Is your leadership increasingly creating peace among your congregation, or are you constantly at odds with those you serve? What about your leadership team or church staff? Is there a peaceful mood in your meetings or does everyone give out a sigh of relief when the meeting comes to an end? I am not saying that we avoid difficult conversation, but to create a peaceful environment that fosters open dialogue in the most strenuous and challenging times. Peace-filled leaders create peaceful teams.

Peace is not always happy and cheerful. If it was, we would all be forced to fake it at times of tragedy. Throughout our season of ministry, there will be multiple seasons of pain created by the brokenness of humanity. You will be called upon to lead God's people throughout these seasons. As God works his righteousness in you, you will bring his peace into these seasons even if your own life is being negatively affected. We can call these seeds of weeping as described in Ps 126:5–6: "Those who sow in tears shall reap with shouts of joy! He who goes out weeping, bearing the seed for sowing, shall come home with shouts of joy, bringing his sheaves with him." The reality of weeping is accompanied by the hopeful promise of restored joy. Don't be afraid to weep or share your deepest feelings with those you lead. I realize that this may be contrary to what you have heard from others, but if Jesus wept, so can we. You may just earn real respect from your congregation by allowing them into your heart even when it is broken. There is peace as we mourn together.

Along with peace, justice is also possible. This is not the worldly justice that looks more like revenge than what the biblical authors had in mind. Proverbs 22:8 comes with an applicable warning as it reads, "Whoever sows injustice will reap calamity, and the rod of his fury will fail." In recent years, many Christians have done a poor job heeding the warning of this proverb. The righteous heart does not look for revenge while calling it justice and using biblical words to promote secular ideologies. Doing so is treading on dangerous ground and should not be accepted within the pastoral ranks. Too many Christian leaders have abused their pulpits to disrupt the peace of the gospel. Refrain from their example and remember that a righteous heart sows seeds of peace and justice.

When you are tempted to seek revenge, calling it justice, remember to pray for wisdom. Proverbs 2:6–8 states, "For the LORD gives wisdom; from his mouth come knowledge and understanding; he stores up sound wisdom for the upright; he is a shield to those who walk in integrity, guarding the paths of justice and watching over the way of his saints." God's wisdom will equip you to guard the paths of justice beginning in your own heart. When this is taking place, you will be able to lead in times of injustice with a heart full of and producing God's righteousness among his people. You and I will not lead in the way of our culture but will transform our communities by planting seeds of righteousness through godly wisdom.

CONCLUDING PRAYER CHALLENGE

We have nothing to sow, until God works righteousness in our hearts through repentance. Until then we have only our self-efforts which usually reflect popular cultural biases. These serve the cultural voice but ignore God's. In this time of prayer, I suggest asking the Holy Spirit to search your heart. Maximizing this time will include returning to your place of prayer with a notepad and pen. Yes, you read that correctly, a notepad and pen. This will relieve you of the temptation of being distracted by your phone or another device. Silently listen to the Holy Spirit, writing everything down that comes to mind. I prefer lists or bullet points. These can then be reviewed and prayed over a multitude of times. Make as many revisions as needed until you sense the peace of having heard from the Lord.

With the peace of the Lord, being assured of his love, make confession. There is no holding back or excuse-making in this process. Be honest with yourself and the Lord. Feel free to write out your confession, or simply allow your heart to speak, making words unnecessary. Often words get in the way of expressing our heart to the Lord. End this time by enjoying his presence. Sit or walk in silence. He is still there, but your sin is not. Your heart has been purified by his Spirit, and you are ready for God's righteousness to produce a harvest.

3

The Seed of the Word of God

WEEK AFTER WEEK, THE word of God pours forth. Local pastors preach from their familiar pulpits to the gathered saints of the church. Many of these sermons took hours to prepare and some nearly an hour to proclaim. Even the smallest churches with limited resources livestream the word of God to online audiences far and wide. If one misses these live events, they have 24/7 access to the messages via YouTube and various podcast providers. Those who love the preaching of their local pastor are also provided with preachers from across the globe. In today's world, there is no shortage of the teaching and preaching of God's word. Ears are full, but are hearts transformed?

Transformation does not come by the constant consumption of the word of God, no more than that one can be made a great musician by simply listening to the best music. At some point, one needs to pick up an instrument and learn to play. In the same way, we who binge our favorite preachers must pick up the word of God and put it into action. Few things encourage the Christian leader more than seeing their messages and teachings put into action in a heart-transforming fashion. When lives are transformed, leaders come alive with enthusiasm and vitality that drives them back into their studies to be led by the Spirit of God in crafting the next lesson.

If life transformation matched the increasing availability of the word of God, I do not believe we would be experiencing the current high level of congregational decline. It has become apparent to the most casual observer that gathering at the church is decreasingly vital to many. I must admit that gathering is pointless if all we gather for is to listen. Pastor, is your goal to get people in the room to listen to you preach? Is that what gives you significance? If so, why would anyone bother? The gathering of the church is not to affirm our ability as public speakers. Our worth to the church is not how many listen but what the listener does with what they hear.

If a thousand people gathered to hear you speak on a Sunday morning, how would you know if it did any good? Can you determine if anyone applied the message to their life? Pastors cannot see the significance or effectiveness of their preaching if they don't try to spend time with their listeners. In the smaller church, pastors have the opportunity to sit face to face with those who listen to them preach, gaining insight into how their messages are being received and applied. This is one reason I am not convinced that the goal should be to increase attendance. That goal tells us how many are listening. It does not reveal if the message did any good. We will do well to proclaim the word of God for the sake of transformation and the maturation of the disciples of Jesus. When we do, the size of the crowd becomes irrelevant. Big or small, those who gather should be growing in Christlikeness, not simply in number.

Before we get lost in the numbers game and I lose your attention, let us consider the words of Jas 1:22–25. In this applicable passage, we see the point that I am trying to make. James writes, "But be doers of the Word, and not hearers only, deceiving yourselves. For if anyone is a hearer of the Word and not a doer, he is like a man who looks intently at his natural face in a mirror. For he looks at himself and goes away and at once forgets what he was like. But the one who looks into the perfect law, the law of liberty, and perseveres, being no hearer who forgets but a doer who acts, he will be blessed in his doing."

Because this book is written primarily for leaders, this passage is not new nor contains difficult or divisive doctrine. We all know it well; most have preached it at least once. We have taught this passage in varying contexts, yet those claiming to have a biblical worldview ignore it and much of the Bible. This is one of the most serious issues Christians face. Ignoring the Bible is creating significant problems in the church and hindering the effectiveness of discipleship and evangelism. As I have stated, the lack of sound teaching is not the problem. The application of our tremendous knowledge is what will bring the desired transformation.

Pastor, I know you are saturating yourself in the word of God every week. You are to be commended for your dedicated study. Week after week, you pour out your heart to the congregation to the point where you want to retreat to your office and enjoy the silence. Sitting in silence, you want to have the reassurance that God is pleased, and you delivered his message to his people. I wish that were enough to help us rest well. However, often it is not. Even in God's pleasure, you think of those who just heard you preach. Will they obey the word of God? Will they apply it to their daily lives? This can keep you up at night and rob you of resting in a job well done. One way to turn this around is to pray specifically for your congregation before preaching and leave the answer to them and the Lord once the message has been delivered.

In my early days of ministry, I was terrified that I would not have enough to say, leaving my sermons too short. Every Sunday, I hoped the worship leader would elongate songs and say lengthy prayers so the service would last the scheduled hour. This anxiety caused me to pray, "Lord, if you don't help me, we will both look stupid." Perhaps I figured God did not want to look stupid, so I pressured him. It was not good theology, but he was gracious, and his Spirit empowered me. Not long before I developed the need to pray, "Lord, teach me how to keep my sermons from being too long." All these years later, I still prayed similar prayers. Hopefully, they are more mature and theologically sound. The remainder of this chapter attempts to help you develop your prayer that will lead to the seed of God's word being deeply planted in the hearts and minds of those you lead. Transformation is the goal.

TEACH THE WORD OF GOD IN SUCH A WAY THAT IT PRODUCES AND TRANSFERS LIFE IN AND THROUGH YOU

Matthew 13:1–9

1 That same day Jesus went out of the house and sat beside the sea. 2
And great crowds gathered about him, so that he got into a boat and
sat down. And the whole crowd stood on the beach. 3 And he told
them many things in parables, saying: "A sower went out to sow. 4 And
as he sowed, some seeds fell along the path, and the birds came and
devoured them. 5 Other seeds fell on rocky ground, where they did not
have much soil, and immediately they sprang up, since they had no
depth of soil, 6 but when the sun rose they were scorched. And since
they had no root, they withered away. 7 Other seeds fell among thorns,
and the thorns grew up and choked them. 8 Other seeds fell on good
soil and produced grain, some a hundredfold, some sixty, some thirty.
9 He who has ears, let him hear."

The prayer that I want to help us develop is based on the parable of the sower. We are at the point in Jesus' ministry when the religious leaders were seeking to destroy him. Because of this, his family was concerned for his well-being. His works and teachings were undeniable, but he did not fit the anticipation of many, and his family thought he was going insane. As he traveled, he spoke about the type of heart that would grasp and be shaped by truth. In Matt 13, he did so, as was his custom. Read Matthew's recollection of the parable and ask the Holy Spirit to bring members of your congregation to mind. This is not done with a judgmental spirit but a pastoral heart.

JESUS SPOKE IN PARABLES BECAUSE IT WAS THE SIMPLEST WAY TO COMMUNICATE TO THOSE WITH RECEPTIVE HEARTS

MATTHEW 13:10–17

10 Then the disciples asked, "Why do you speak to them in parables?"

11 And he answered them, "To you it has been given to know the
secrets of the kingdom of heaven, but to them it has not been given.
12 For to the one who has, more will be given, and he will have an
abundance, but from the one who has not, even what he has will be
taken away. 13 This is why I speak to them in parables, because seeing
they do not see, and hearing they do not hear, nor do they understand.
14 Indeed, in their case the prophecy of Isaiah is fulfilled that says: 'You
will indeed hear but never understand, and you will indeed see but
never perceive. 15 For this people's heart has grown dull, and with their
ears they can barely hear, and their eyes they have closed, lest they
should see with their eyes and hear with their ears and understand
with their heart and turn, and I would heal them.' 16 But blessed are
your eyes, for they see, and your ears, for they hear. 17 For truly, I say
to you, many prophets and righteous people longed to see what you
see, and did not see it, and to hear what you hear, and did not hear it."

Jesus chose to reveal the secretes of the kingdom of heaven to those who desired to learn, keeping truth away from those whose heart had grown dull. That is, they were unwilling to believe. It's not that Jesus was keeping the truth away from those seeking it with their whole hearts. The truth of God's word is withheld from those who close their hearts and minds. God does not force anyone to believe. Truth is reserved for those with receptive hearts. Therefore, he spoke in parables.

As you think about the congregation you serve, some with dull hearts may come to mind. The condition of their heart is the result of willful ignorance. They have closed their eyes and refuse to obey the word of God, choosing to follow the dictates of their mind. Week after week, they listen to your sermons and remain untransformed. The temptation is to blame yourself, thinking that if you were a better preacher, these individuals would experience the life-changing benefits of the word of God. You could be the most gifted communicator in the church's history yet have untransformed listeners. The power is in the word, not your performance on the platform.

Reality is revealed by the apostle John when he stated, "And this is the judgment: the light has come into the world, and people loved the darkness rather than the light because their works were evil" (John 3:19). I understand this to be a difficult thing to consider when thinking about your congregation, but let it sink in. Those who want untransformed lives will hide in the darkness of willful ignorance. They do not wish to tell the truth. They seek only affirmation of their ideas. The crowds that followed Jesus were packed with these people and sit within our congregations.

All hope is not lost; we can be encouraged by the nature of God's word and the work of his Holy Spirit. These two aspects of our discipleship are at work in many. Those who desire transformational truth receive the same sermons and words of counsel rejected by the dull-hearted. For these saints of the church, we are to help them develop a heart that seeks to understand. Their heart to learn is fuel for your heart to shepherd. As they seek transformation, we can help them in many ways. *I suggest two ways to do so here.*

To launch those under your care towards receiving transformative truth, model and guide them away from willful ignorance. Will ignorance fill the heart of the fearful who seek to avoid the accountability of knowledge? They dodge the responsibility of practice and obedience if they don't know. This may be one reason for avoiding new ideas among many of our most consistent church attendees. They seek to hear the same familiar teaching to keep living the same familiar lifestyle. Helping them reject willful ignorance will be a significant step forward in Christian discipleship, opening a new pathway to understanding truth.

A second suggestion is to reject the postmodern idea that truth is subjective. Today, this idea is part of the air we breathe. Sunday after Sunday, those listening to the teachings of the Bible instinctively filter what they hear through their subjective lens. Many will listen from the position that what you teach as biblical is your subjective interpretation, and if their understanding is different, so be it. If this is not corrected, your leadership will be rendered ineffective, and discipleship will not occur through your ministry. To shed further light on this issue, consider that your listeners filter much of what they hear through their preconceived notions and emotions. They must navigate these to open their hearts and minds toward learning the truth as revealed in Scripture and consistent with reality.

These two suggestions will help you lead from an epistemologically sound position. Your investigation and presentation on truth claims will be what distinguishes your leadership. Without them, your manner of leading will be silenced by the noise of opinions rushing through the minds of your congregants, who see the world through their self-justified ideas. To be an effective leader, your voice must rise above the cultural noise through the power of the Holy Spirit and the authority of God's word. When you commit to this, God will guide you to receptive hearts into which you will boldly speak. If you are ready to commit, pause your reading and converse with the Lord.

WHAT KIND OF LISTENER ARE YOU

MATTHEW 13:18–23

18 Hear then the parable of the sower: 19 When anyone hears the Word
of the kingdom and does not understand it, the evil one comes and
snatches away what has been sown in his heart. This is what was sown
along the path. 20 As for what was sown on rocky ground, this is the
one who hears the Word and immediately receives it with joy, 21 yet
he has no root in himself but endures for a while. When tribulation or

persecution arises on account of the Word, he immediately falls away.
22 As for what was sown among thorns, this is the one who hears the
Word, but the cares of the world and the deceitfulness of riches choke
the Word, proving unfruitful. 23 As for what was sown on good soil,
this is the one who hears the Word and understands it. He indeed
bears fruit and yields, in one case a hundredfold, in another sixty, and
in another thirty.

Understanding why Jesus used parables as the best way to shape receptive hearts prepares us to understand the next section of the biblical text. In verses eighteen through twenty-three, Jesus revealed four basic types of listeners. Parables were and continue to be an effective means of communication for those ready to receive and become fruitful through application. We may wish everyone under our care to be in such a state. Imagine if you preached to crowds of people every Sunday, ready to be transformed by God's word and move out into their relational Word to transfer life and growth. This would make the ministry much more enjoyable. Sadly, reality is very different because many who listen are unprepared to hear.

Some of those unprepared to hear and produce fruit listen to you while confused. Not only do they not understand your message at the moment, but they are also confused about the Christian life. Those sitting in the pews or connecting with your teaching through various platforms often lack a basic understanding of the biblical narrative and what Jesus came to accomplish. Sit back and think about your congregation. Hopefully, some are just starting to investigate what Christianity is and have no knowledge other than culture speak. Others may have a mosaic of religious ideologies, thinking they are all valid.

Additionally, present within most congregations are the well-trained and theologically astute, who judge everything you say by their preferred system of theology. My holding to the Wesleyan-Holiness perspective can confuse those raised in a Calvinistic setting. Knowing what may sound confusing to your congregation is essential if you want to help them become fruit-bearing learners.

The confused listener is not the only person sitting in the pews. Sitting right next to them is the easily discouraged listener. They quickly meet you after the service, saying how much they benefited from the sermon. However, Monday comes, bringing the first challenges of the week, negating any positive growth spawned the previous day. We can trivialize this with our listeners' daily grind and short memories, thinking that Jesus said this is how it will be. But, this will be a disservice to all involved. Instead, we can shape our sermons to include encouraging practical steps for the upcoming week. I end every sermon with a personal challenge and a corporate vision. For your quickly discouraged listeners, cast a vision for what can be.

Our next type of listener may be called the crowded listener. They lack the necessary space to apply what they receive. Showing up with the best intentions and looking for relief, they listen to the sermon. No matter how hard they try or what promise they make, their hearts are too crowded. They often need to off-load their emotional and spiritual baggage. Would they do well to worship in song and then leave the service? Sound strange? Perhaps it is. However, when the psalmist poured out their heart, did they then listen to a sermon? People don't always need to hear but must be listened to. Maybe they need to come to church to drop off some stuff with the Lord and get some things off their chest. Think it through; it may make sense.

Finally, we have the listener that we all want to teach. The fruitful listener is our favorite congregant. They hear, understand, and bear fruit. What percentage of our listeners are this type? If the 80/20 rule applies here, we have about 20 percent of our congregation in the fruitful category. If you are discouraged by this, read through one of the Gospel accounts to see how Jesus was received as he taught. Though his crowds were huge, they were mixed for sure. Or reflect on how Paul the apostle was received. He tended to start riots. Thinking about Jesus and Paul is enough. Don't venture back to the Old Testament prophets because most of them were killed for speaking on God's behalf. One thing we can do is prepare and deliver sermons that address each type of listener.

Your congregation and mine are filled with confused, discouraged, crowded listeners that we hope become fruitful. With the Lord's help, it can be done.

CONCLUDING PRAYER CHALLENGE

Few things breathe satisfaction into our inner being as Christian leaders more than seeing those under our care become fruit-bearing doers of God's word. Seeing our dedication to teaching the Bible come alive to our learners encourages and inspires perseverance in the pulpit. The opposite is equally deflating and uninspiring. With all we have said in this chapter, the challenge becomes to pray that the seed of God's word produces life in those willing to listen. The basis for this prayer is believing his powerful Word generates and transfers life and growth. Stepping into this prayer challenge, we petition God to give us the ability to share his word in the most basic, understandable forms. Like Jesus did with the use of parables, we are to do this today.

We are also to pray that God would guide us to those seeking to understand. Watch and listen for the Spirit's prompting as people approach you with questions about your teachings. Questions are signs of God's prevenient grace. As we pray, the seed of his word will create life where there has been only death and chaos.

4

The Seed of Faith

MANY BIBLICAL PASSAGES ON faith leave the reader somewhat discouraged and require further reflection, prayer, and contemplation. Miracle stories fit into this category. Discouragement stems from the reality that, by definition, miracles are rare. They are suspensions of the norm, pointing to a spiritual truth. In other words, the miracles themselves were rarely, if ever, the point of their inclusion in the Gospel narrative. Their purpose pointed to Jesus' identity and power over the spirit world, the natural world, and ultimately life and death. In short, miracles are signposts, and signs can be confusing. Imagine yourself attempting to navigate an unfamiliar city full of signs you do not understand. That is the reality for many Christians who tried to navigate the teachings of the Bible and place their faith in Jesus.

Biblical passages containing miracles are not only difficult to understand but also discouraging for those who pray for a miracle and don't receive the answer they so desperately desire. They see Jesus healing many in the Bible, but not themselves or their loved ones today. This gives rise to a struggle to maintain their faith in Jesus and the Bible. After a season of prolonged disappointment, these passages become reasons for abandoning faith and adopting the belief that Christianity is false or something worse. Honest Christians admit and embrace the struggle.

In Matt 19:20, we have one of the most challenging examples. Here, Jesus is recorded as saying, "For truly, I say to you, if you have faith like a grain of mustard seed, you will say to this mountain, 'Move from here to there,' and it will move, and nothing will be impossible for you." The initial response of many is, *Yeah right!* They find many things impossible and are 100 percent convinced that some things will never be what they want them to be. They once believed, but what they prayed for did not become what they experienced. This is catastrophic for those who now live with shattered faith.

As a leader, you can see why many statements made by Jesus are difficult for the people under your care. You are the one they come to seeking prayer and support. You show up, read Scripture, offer words of encouragement, and join them in prayer. As you do, your weaknesses and struggles become vivid in your mind, though they are not present in your words. As you say the appropriate things to those seeking your help, your heart may not be one with your words. As a Christian leader, you know that God can do whatever he desires. You just don't understand why he does not. We know he can, but we don't always understand why he has not. This is where the leader's faith is revealed and tested. I pray that you find help by digging a bit deeper into the text. As we do, I am asking God to help us understand that . . .

A SMALL AMOUNT OF RIGHTLY PLACED FAITH CAN GENERATE AND TRANSFER LIFE AND GROWTH

Matthew 17:14–21

14 And when they came to the crowd, a man came up to him and,
kneeling before him, 15 said, "Lord, have mercy on my son, for he is
an epileptic and he suffers terribly. For often he falls into the fire, and
often into the water. 16 And I brought him to your disciples, and they

could not heal him." 17 And Jesus answered, "O faithless and twisted
generation, how long am I to be with you? How long am I to bear
with you? Bring him here to me." 18 And Jesus rebuked the demon,
and it came out of him, and the boy was healed instantly. 19 Then the
disciples came to Jesus privately and said, "Why could we not cast it
out?" 20 He said to them, "Because of your little faith. For truly, I say to
you, if you have faith like a grain of mustard seed, you will say to this
mountain, 'Move from here to there,' and it will move, and nothing will
be impossible for you."

THE DIFFICULTY OF NECESSITY FOR LEADERS TO RIGHTLY PLACE THEIR FAITH

Most of the people we lead experience the pain of suffering loved ones. This is especially painful when the loved one is a child. Pastoring those dealing with this type of pain will be some of the most difficult times we face. They will also be some of the most remarkable seasons of participating in the power of the Holy Spirit. As the Comforter, he operates through us as we are present with the hurting. The faith of the hurting may be small, but as you continue to show up full of the Holy Spirit, life and growth will transform the heart of the hurting.

A second reality makes our ministry to the hurting even more challenging. Our faith becomes part of the solution or the problem. Note in verse 16 that the man with the epileptic boy tells Jesus that he brought his son to the disciples, but they were unable to heal him. Unfortunately, this is a common prayer. People bring us their painful issues, and we are unable to help. We then feel incapable and doubt concerning our call begins to rise. This is especially difficult for young pastors. They may not have the experience to deal with such a blow to the leadership's confidence.

Moving forward in the text, we see a third difficulty. Jesus can become disappointed with us as we operate without faith in the care of others. Notice the tone of verse 17. Jesus refers to his disciples as "faithless and twisted." These are difficult and convicting words. As I read them, I reflect on people under my care who are not growing or moving forward in faith. I contemplate the words of Jesus, asking the Holy Spirit to search my heart and reveal any possible faithlessness in me. Many times, we are the problem, but not always. Allow the ministry of the Holy Spirit to encourage or convict you concerning your role in the lives of the hurting. You are probably doing better than you think.

If you are a leader who is too quick to assign blame or responsibility, remember that Jesus does not always do what he did in this passage. Yes, he healed this boy and continues to heal many today. However, the majority of those following Jesus do not experience miracles of healing until they are glorified in eternity. This is because eternal healing and Jesus' power over death were the typical purposes of healing miracles. Remember, each recorded miracle was a sign pointing to a larger reality. Recorded miracles were not promises that everyone would experience on this side of heaven. Each of these miracles was temporary, and their recipients eventually experienced physical death. We all do.

The final two verses of this text create three more specific challenges. There are times in our leadership that Jesus will reveal our lack of faith. We can sink into a sense of hopelessness, believing that some things are simply impossible to achieve. The opposite seems to be Jesus' point as he compares the size of our faith with that of our problem. Our faith may be small, but the problem is significant; yet, nothing is impossible. Small faith can bring life and growth, offering solutions to even the most pressing issues. The biggest of all may be times when God says no to our request for a miracle. With just a little faith, we can navigate our most significant problems because our faith is in God's wisdom and power, which is not without mystery. Do we put our faith in God even when he says no?

A SMALL AMOUNT OF RIGHTFULLY PLACED FAITH GENERATES AND TRANSFERS LIFE AND GROWTH

With the above difficulties acknowledged, we need not stop there in befuddlement. We may not understand every aspect of how faith operates, but our trust is in the Lord and his wisdom. Remember that exercising our faith is less about what we ask and more about who we are addressing in prayer. Trusting him allows us to make our requests known to him with complete confidence that he will act according to his divine will. When operating in this manner of faith, all things become possible, including thriving when his answer is not what we desired. That is leading in true faith.

Circling back to the beginning of our text, we see in verse 14 a common occurrence in ministry circles. The soil in which the seed begins to grow is often the failure of faithlessness. As a leader, many will come to you with long-standing issues that the Lord has not yet dealt with, expressing the inability of other Christians to make any difference. At the same time, many will leave your church, accusing you of being faithless to the point of failure. Those who move from church to church often do so with unresolved hurts and spiritual challenges. Based on our immediate text, this movement can be the result of faithless leadership.

As challenging as faithless leadership may be, remember that even when you are ministering in complete faith, you may be accused of the opposite because God does say no to our requests. This is a multilayered and complicated theological issue. I am only addressing a small piece here. Apply this small part to your ministry as you consider the connected biblical doctrines. For now, when those expressing the perceived failure of others arrive, place your faith in the wisdom and character of God. Doing so will assure that faith generates and transfers life and growth even when it is planted in the soil of faithless failure.

In addition to faithlessness, Jesus' authority over the spirit world forms the context of our discussion. There is much mystery to this area of theology. Demonology is a prevalent biblical issue, yet speaking of it today seems extreme to many. Although there is much disagreement in this area, one thing is clear. All authority has been given to Jesus. In fact, throughout the New Testament, demons have a much better grasp on this reality than the disciples of Jesus. May I remind you that you are a spiritual leader and operate in the spirit world, whether you fully comprehend it or not? Faith in Jesus' authority over demonic spirits is essential for those leading in the church today. Embrace and trust Jesus as you lead, shedding light in the darkness.

As faith generates and transfers life and growth in the seedbed of faithlessness and demonic oppression, Jesus is patient. He bears with us in the faithless twisting of reality. Trusting in his patience and forbearance, we can lean in to his grace. His grace is in his conviction. In verse 17 of our text, he displays this with the question of "How long?" How long does he have to be with us and us with him before we lead in faithful witness? As a pastor for nearly thirty years, this question plagues me.

If this question has the same effect on you, let us join together in prayer that our faith would grow to at least the size of a mustard seed. As leaders, today, we have some central mountains to move and there is no time for faithless leadership. We live in a twisted world, where every moral and spiritual thread is being woven into knots of anxiety and depression. Thankfully, Jesus is not setting a tremendously high bar. He is asking for at least a small faith. Can we at least offer him that much and challenge our congregation to the same? I believe we can and must. There is no room for faithless leadership, and quitting is not a better option. It seems to me that sowing seeds of faith is the only way forward.

LEADING BY EXERCISING GENERATIVE AND TRANSFORMING FAITH

Generative and transforming faith is exercised by walking in the authority given to us by Jesus. A closer look at our text reveals a poignant leadership question. Why were they hindered by "little faith" when all Jesus said they needed was "faith like a grain of mustard seed"? To answer this question, we require some textual clarity. The phrase "little faith" is more accurately translated as "poor faith." With this clarification, Jesus' words make more sense to today's reader. The issue for the disciples who failed to help the boy and his father was the poor quality of their faith. Faith can be small and effective, but a large amount of poor faith can create catastrophic leadership failure. This is a poignant way to suggest that stupidity can undermine leadership and ministry effectiveness. You know what I am talking about because we have all made decisions in complete, unabashed confidence that only led to disaster. Thankfully, Jesus bailed us out, just as he did the disciples in our text.

To gain a further understanding of our question through textual clarity, we must return to chapter 10 of Matthew's Gospel. Doing so reveals a bit more about their failure to bring healing to the boy in question. Their failure, recorded in chapter 17, is due to their inability to exercise the authority given to them by Jesus faithfully. In Matt 10:1, Jesus "called to him his twelve disciples and gave them authority over unclean spirits, to cast them out, and to heal every disease and every affliction." Could this be the reason Jesus seemed disappointed with the disciples? Is this poor faith? If so, it can also be a serious issue for leaders today.

As leaders, we need to exercise our God-given authority. The seed of faith will only do its work when we do. False humility and fear will keep us from this vital leadership requirement. In my denomination and many others like it, ordained elders are charged with leading and feeding their congregations. This does not mean that we lead from the top down, but often from the bottom up. I like to call this the authoritative servant, serving our churches and communities by exercising the authority of Jesus. If you are a leader, then lead with faith and authority.

CONCLUDING PRAYER CHALLENGE

With all that I have addressed about faith as a seed that transfers life and growth, the challenge becomes asking for help when our belief is overshadowed by unbelief. Although asking for help is difficult for many leaders, it is the honest vulnerability required for progress. The father's request for a miracle from Jesus in Mark 9 is a suitable example. He admits that his faith is mixed with a lack of it when he states, "I believe; help my unbelief!" As leaders, we are encouraged to admit areas of unbelief without condemnation.

This admission and request for help begin with prayer. It amazes me how many leaders attempt to disguise their weaknesses before the Lord. We know better, yet we try to approach his throne of grace with false confidence. This is not necessary through being well motivated. You want to be pleasing to the Lord and, in so doing, attempt to cover your weakness with lofty pastoral language. Give up the façade and open your doubting heart to the Lord. Remember, his throne is one of grace.

5

The Seed of the Unseen Work of the Holy Spirit

STANDING IN THE SMALL church foyer, a space that could not have been bigger than 10 x 10 in the mountains of southwestern Virginia, I waited. I waited for God. I waited for the weekly eight attendees to show up. I waited for any guests who might stumble upon the hidden church tucked away in a neighborhood that had long since forgotten the church. The church had once had dreams of growth and had designed its building to accommodate expansion. However, there was no need during my tenure, as the same eight people attended week after week, and the seed of faith seemed to have all but dried up.

Decades on from that time, when I pause and reflect on that humble tenure, I can still see the two identical sets of glass doors in that small foyer. One set led to the parking lot and a covered pull-through area, while the other set led to an expansive grass area where a future addition could be made. The set of doors that led to the grass area was never opened, as they were doors that would open during a jubilee moment in the church's life, which never came.

Had the seed planted through faith to build the church all but dried up? Had the people been disobedient and failed to cultivate the ground for a future harvest through prayer and fasting? Had God all but forgotten this little wayside church tucked into a neighborhood? Whatever the answer, what kept this band of faithful churchgoers going amid the lack of growth or spiritual momentum? There were always more questions than answers in the small foyer where I stood, week after week, praying and hoping that someone new would come. Mark 4:26–29 speaks to a seed that seemed to be scattered, maybe even thrown about by the seed sower onto the ground, and the supernatural provision of God would provide growth.

Mark 4:26–29

26 He also said, "This is what the kingdom of God is like. A man scat-
ters seed on the ground. 27 Night and day, whether he sleeps or gets
up, the seed sprouts and grows, though he does not know how. 28 All
by itself the soil produces grain—first the stalk, then the head, then the
full kernel in the head. 29 As soon as the grain is ripe, he puts the sickle
to it, because the harvest has come."

THE UNKNOWN SEED

Why do some churches experience growth, while others don't? Why does some people's faith help them overcome significant life challenges, while others give up at the first sign of distress in their lives? Is it a lack of faith? Or a lack of supernatural direction and blessing? Doesn't God love each of us and see our needs? Surely, he is a God of grace who extends a hand of help to each person and situation they face. These and other questions might have gone through your mind in the past or during a trying season of life. It is in the unseen seed that God is working for your good and that of the local church. God is calling you to walk in a seed of faith, not a seed of flesh.

I cannot picture God leaning over the banister of heaven, wondering what should happen to the small church or even to you in your daily walk with him. He formed you in your mother's womb, and he is not surprised by what you face daily. What must be the surprise is that you and I don't understand that the Holy Spirit is with us daily. He guides our path if we would listen. He helps us to overcome difficult situations if we follow his guidance. Did you catch the word "if"? It takes you changing your mindset and walking not in the seen (natural) but the unseen (the supernatural). The Holy Spirit is the unseen seed that is planted inside of you if you would allow him to grow and take charge of your life. This is the legacy gift that Christ gave the world when he ascended into heaven, the gift of walking in the Spirit.

GUIDANCE IN THE SEED

In the passage of Scripture (Mark 4:26–29) that Mark references, Jesus is speaking and reminds the reader that humanity is not built on self, or even selfishness, but on the Savior who asks you to capture the vision for the lost, obey in serving and sharing, and do your part in helping others as you help your own walk with God. There is a level of guidance that the Holy Spirit provides to the seeker if they are willing and able to obey the prompt. God did not promise that the seed scatterer would bear fruit from the seed, but it was the action, the faith, really, that enabled the seed to take hold as the scatterer threw the seed to the ground.

It is in the unseen that the Spirit of God works the best. There is guidance in the seed that comes about when the one who throws (you) and the one who waters and grows (God) work together through trust that the seed can begin to take root and grow. This step takes patience and courage, as time is a precious commodity in growing in faith. It is in the surrendering of your will that God can guide by an unseen or sometimes unfelt force that is called the Holy Spirit. The Spirit of God is a provider who helps daily in your walk to live a life of holiness. Holiness is not unattainable but can be lived when the sower takes hold of the guidance of the Spirit over their life.

OBEYING WITH SEED FAITH

I have spoken to countless pastors and church leaders about their seed faith over the past nearly two decades. While I did not call church revitalization, or leading a comeback church, seed faith, it is. Seed faith is believing in the word, taking it in, and then living out what God has taught through his word. It sounds easy, and perhaps it should be, but sadly, many who start following God or even desire to say yes to God's call fall away over time. Why? The simple answer is a lack of obedience. Obedience is a surrendering of your will to God's will over your life. That means *all* aspects of your life, not just the ones you will give to God.

Let us revisit the Scripture and focus on verse 27 specifically (Mark 4:27): "He sleeps and rises night and day, and the seed sprouts and grows; he knows not how." The final four words are the words you should focus on: "he knows not how." Cross out the word "he" and add your name. You may not know how the seed of faith grows, but you can do your part by being obedient to the call. Obedience has more to do with self than the Savior, as you have to allow yourself to let go and let God take hold of all aspects of your life. And if you are honest, that is tough. Obedience is full surrender. It's a freedom from you trying to control everything in your life and working with a partner (God) in negotiating the path you are traveling.

The seed scatterer (you) and God make a powerful team if you understand that you are subordinate to God and not the other way around. When the scatterer of the seed does their part, scatter seed, sleep, and rise again, the Lord can do his part and provide a harvest to come. You want a harvest, I know you do, or you would not be reading this resource. But, here is the question: Will I do my part in God's plan, or will I get in the way? So, what will it be? Will you obey?

THE SEED OF THE HARVEST

When you surrender to the will and calling that God has for you, you begin to see things through his eyes. The eyes of the Lord see your life and ministry differently than you do. He sees ten paces ahead, whereas you see only the first step. The question is: Will you reach the harvest, or give up before you arrive? Far too many have given up long before they experience the supernatural move of God over their lives. Let us refocus on the Scripture, specifically on verse 29, which states, "As soon as the grain is ripe, he puts the sickle to it, because the harvest has come."

The first seven words should capture your spiritual imagination: "As soon as the grain is ripe . . ." God does not want to wait to provide for you; he wants to do it right away. The problem is not him; it's you. It's us. It's humanity pushing back against his plan and his desires for your local ministry and walk with him. You must transition from a "feeling" about your relationship with God to "knowing" that he is with you and in you. God has called you to walk out your faith daily. He has not called you to hide your faith in the workplace or in other environments, such as being an undercover Christian. No, he has asked, maybe even challenged, to live out your faith from the morning until you go to bed at night. Faith is not just a Sunday attire that you put on and take off when the service is over. Faith is a spiritually ingrained, DNA-like quality, one that lives with God daily.

When others begin to see your faith lived out in all the circumstances of life, they start to seek the "why" behind the "what." They might ask, "Why are you happy when difficulties come? And what is the relationship you have with Jesus?" It is there that your faith can be shared, relationships of trust built, and the seeds that are sown can be harvested in the near future.

THE HARVEST TOOLS

God is calling you to harvest the fields that are before you. In layman's terms, God is calling you to win people to Jesus in the community where you live. If you are like me, you might feel overwhelmed by the prospects and feel like an imposter when you try. Imposter syndrome has affected many of us, making us feel like a fraud at work. Yet, we are not frauds in God's eyes. He has equipped, gifted, and called you for such a time as this to reach your coworker, neighbor, or friend with the gospel. What a daunting task, but a rewarding one, nonetheless. So, reflect and ask yourself: What is in my hands? God has placed the right "tools" in your life through life experiences and spiritual connectedness to reach people around you with the gospel.

Let us go back and look at verse 29: "he puts the sickle to the harvest . . ." The word "sickle" might distract you. The sickle is a tool to harvest a crop. A sharp tool that slices and cuts through the harvest in the field. That is what you are in God's hands. A tool to connect with the community around you to share about him. If you are like most people, you might feel uncomfortable as a tool for the Lord. He calls you to speak to people who don't look so friendly. He stretches you to bake bread for a neighbor who has been so cross with your family. He asks you to help the coworker who does everything to undermine you. Yes, he sees. He sees your potential, and the spiritual growth that can take place if you allow yourself to be used by God.

The sickle is a sharp tool that can cut through the most forbidding field. Do not allow fear of the unknown to keep you from what God already knows, and as you remember, you have been birthed for such a time as this. Capture not the imagination of uncertainty but capture the heart of Christ to use your giftings to capture the moment you have been called into.

GOING INTO THE HARVEST FIELDS

So, we have talked about calling and serving; now, let's look at where you can connect to the community. Many times, people think it's a program or another person's responsibility to reach someone else. But, in this case, God is calling you to be that person and, in turn, use his simple plan to win the harvest by meeting them right where they are found. Let's call this program "God blessed." The God-blessed program is simple; it's a way of serving others that will connect you with the person God has called you to communicate with. The God-blessed program is praying intentionally, focusing remotely, and serving in the community.

Praying Intentionally

Who has God laid on your heart? What name comes up as a prompting of the Holy Spirit to your heart and mind even now? God is bringing these names to mind because he wants you to pray for them. Focusing your heart and mind on where God might have you serve in the community is also focusing on what God has for your ministry. Yes, ministry. You are called to serve even when you are not the pastor. Sometimes that means connecting with a co-worker or a client at work or praying about opportunities to serve at a local nonprofit or in your local church. The idea is to be open to what God has for you and is calling you to in the near future by spending time in consistent prayer throughout the day or by setting aside time to routinely commune with God.

Focusing Remotely

Each day, you are bombarded with actions that the world is asking you to make. While some actions are simple, like deciding which shirt to wear for an important client meeting or what to eat for lunch, other actions challenge you to pause and think. It is in these pause moments, when focusing remotely—removing yourself from self and observing the situation through Christ's eyes—that you begin to see the need, the request, or the action that must be taken. This takes a prayerful spirit to be open to these God-prompts. As you go throughout your day, who is the Spirit guiding you to? Who is the Spirit asking you to slow down and engage with? When you refocus your priorities on God, you begin to see more and more where God is moving you to obey and follow.

Serving in the Community

As you drive to work or church during the week, what do you see around you? Blight, hardship, struggle? These are areas where God is calling his people to serve. You might live in a nice neighborhood or work in a high-rise, but God is calling you to humble yourself and serve the downtrodden of the world. This forgotten class is where God is calling the church and you specifically to minister to those who have been affected by life circumstances. When you give a piece of your time as part of a hands-on service project or nonprofit, you are investing not only in the ones you are helping but also in your own spiritual walk. In these unguarded times where you serve in the community, God uses these times to inspire, encourage, and renew your own heart to see more freely as you see others around you. Consider prayerfully a place where you could give to others what Christ has given to you.

SHARE THE HARVEST WITH OTHERS

If you are reading this book, then you are on a journey of faith. As you go deeper and deeper with God, you have a wonderful opportunity to share that renewing faith with others. I love the closing words of this passage of Scripture that we have been studying this chapter: "because the harvest has come." I have pondered these closing words repeatedly and even got stuck on what to write next because they are so powerful. If the "harvest has come," what are you supposed to do? Good question. The simple answer is: share it with others. God is calling you, maybe even commanding you as a Christian, to share the "good news" with others. Stop and think about how many people you come in contact with daily. Those are the folks that God is asking you to share your faith with. Yes, I know it's uncomfortable and maybe even hard, but they should have the joy that you have in living and serving God daily.

Far too many Christians keep their faith to themselves and do not show it. It's heartbreaking to think that faith-filled Christians have the gift, but they choose not to share the gift of faith with others. Do not allow others to say that about you. Be bold. Be actionable. Be a harvester who shares their faith not as a badge of honor, but as a loving gift that you can extend to others. In the end, when you live out your faith, others will see not you (insert your name here), but they will see Jesus in and through you.

CONCLUDING PRAYER CHALLENGE

Spend time in prayer seeking those whom God is calling you to help in their spiritual walk. Find time to disconnect from the world so you can connect with God by listening to his still small voice, leaning in to what he may be saying, and allowing the Spirit to guide you forward in sharing from a posture of humility and love for others the warmth of the Lord.

Put aside ten minutes today to sit still and alone with God, allowing him to speak with you about next steps as you claim the harvest that is before you. God has a plan for your life, but will you allow him to use you?

6

The Seed of the Kingdom of God

The Now and Not Yet of God Rule in the World

Some years back, a small Bible caught my eye while walking through a used bookstore in Louisville, Kentucky. It was small, well worn, and stuck out amongst the larger Bible printings in the aisle. Pausing and picking up the Bible, I naturally flipped to the opening pages, searching for the copyright date. Within the pages of every book, there is always a story ready to be told, and for me, I looked just inside to see where the story of this Bible began. What surprised me was not the copyright date, but the handwritten inscription found just inside the first couple of pages. Typically, I would not want a book, much less a Bible, to have writing I did not place in it, but there it was, one beautifully written sentence that sent my mind tracing back the history of those simple but special words with a series of unanswered questions in my mind.

"MAY 27, 1957, TO FAITH, FROM MOMMY AND DADDY"

My mind whirled for a few seconds, caught in unanswered questions. Who was Faith? How did such a sentimental Bible come into a used bookstore? How old was Faith when given this Bible? Did Faith lose the Bible or lose her faith? I was reminded again that a story is told behind every word written on the page. In May 1957, a mother and father gifted their little girl a Bible as a reminder that Faith is not just her name but a lifestyle to live out with Christ throughout her life. From the beginning, stories have been passed orally, artistically, and in written form. Today, with the onset of new emerging technologies, storytelling is being transformed even as I write this. Still, one fundamental fact remains, that inside everyone is a story yearning to be told.

Throughout the ages, shared stories have been tweaked, half forgotten, or distorted to fit a new narrative of time and place, often missing the originator's original intent. But not so with the story of God. The treasured stories found in the Bible are living, breathing examples of what was, what is, and what will be. What is remarkable is that even as time has marched on, the story of God has never shifted or changed with time. It is the one thing that has stayed constant. While leaders of all stripes have tried to pervert and subvert the meaning of God's word, throughout the centuries, his word has remained firm and unbending to the sin-natured world it was birthed into. The seed of redemption and salvation has not wavered nor changed in the shifting political, relational, or geographical alliances. The seed of the kingdom of God will hold until we reach eternity.

THE COMPREHENSIVE YET OFTEN HARD-TO-SEE SPREAD OF GOD'S RULE

Mark 4:30–33

30 Again he said, "What shall we say the kingdom of God is like, or

what parable shall we use to describe it? 31 It is like a mustard seed,
which is the smallest of all seeds on earth. 32 Yet when planted,
it grows and becomes the largest of all garden plants, with such
big branches that the birds can perch in its shade." 33 With many
similar parables Jesus spoke the word to them, as much as they could
understand.

In the world you've grown up in (your neighborhood, city, or state), and the world that has shaped your spiritual faith (discipleship, church, or denomination), these two worlds, when they collide, can cause real questions for the faithful follower. Perhaps you have felt the tug-of-war that occurs between the world you know and the world you are growing into. This battle that takes place between the physical and spiritual directs the self toward the Savior, both in the present and in the future, but it is hard as you cling to the mustard seed faith you begin with.

KINGDOM BUILDING ON EARTH

There is a brewing battle in neighborhoods, states, and countries where land becomes the power base of a person, government, or nation. It inflates land over a person in the value of "community." It separates the wealthy and people experiencing poverty, builds class systems in the workplace, and derides a lack of education compared to those who have completed a college degree. These seeds of inequity have been seen since the fall in the garden of Eden and have cast a long shadow of sin over the world ever since, where power and prestige take precedence over grace, love, and hope is found in Scripture. The world created by God has transformed into a sin-filled lust, a lust-filled world driven not by the sanctity of Scripture but by the sin-captured reality that more is a must and not less is more.

Scripture records in Mark 4:31, "It is like a mustard seed, which is the smallest of all seeds on earth." Did you catch the keyword in this passage of Scripture, "smallest"? Think about it this way: what can God do with the smallest prayer in your life?

What could God do with the smallest problem in your life? What could God do to solve the smallest burden on your heart? The reality is a lot. Yet, many followers and non-followers focus on world solutions and miss what the spiritual can do. The fact is that kingdom building has taken a firm hold in the fabric of a person's life. Instead of rejecting the world, the world has seeped within the church and taken hold of its members who search for worldly solutions to their spiritual problems.

In this passage of Scripture, there is a seed of what comes next when a person focuses on God. Mark 4:32 says, "Yet when planted, it grows and becomes the largest of all garden plants, with such big branches the birds can perch in its shade." Maybe you are like me and have never seen a mustard plant. So, I did a quick Google search to see an image and read more about the seed. The seed of this plant is tiny, perhaps even minuscule, compared to other seeds that can be planted in a garden. But this mighty seed can grow into something extraordinary. The small seed grows into a tree. The massive tree takes up space larger and broader than one can imagine. That is what the kingdom of God can do outside the realm of the world. Sin keeps the seeds of people's faith small, and followers are not able to see the potential they are holding inside their hearts. But, when that seed (a believer's life) is given over to the Lord, the seed becomes planted, watered, fed, and transformation takes place. Here is the remarkable thing that happens: a God-size tree springs forth.

KINGDOM BUILDING IN THE SPIRIT

Words have a transformational power that transcends time and space. Words spoken or written down can impact a person or their family for generations. In Mark 4:30–33, Jesus uses storytelling to tell the ways of God. He creatively uses what is familiar to the hearers to understand the sometimes cumbersome understanding of what God shares through his word, the Bible. The Bible, written by man and inspired by God, has transformed lives through the impact of the written page centuries after it was shared, and it connects the Spirit with the soul inside each person. The kingdom of God means nothing unless the person hearing the word receives and then allows the words to transform their heart and soul.

Mark 4:33 says, "With many similar parables Jesus spoke the word to them, as much as they could understand." Maybe you are like me and did not know what a mustard seed looked like, or had never seen one grow from seed into tree form, but the people in Jesus' time did. The stories that Jesus shared helped ordinary people connect daily reality with the extraordinary thought that Christ had come for them. That through his death and resurrection, there could be so much more for the world's lost. The story that Jesus was sharing drew the listener in, but it's only when hearing becomes sight that lives are transformed with the gospel message of the "good news."

When the kingdom message of grace, hope, love, and forgiveness penetrates the heart of the sin-filled soul, transformational life through sanctification occurs. Here, Jesus shared a simple truth that radically affected the listeners' lives. The ruler over their hearts would transform from an earthly, even worldly ruler to one of creation itself, God. The soul is the significant component of what Christ was trying to reach as he connected a modern object through storytelling to the kingdom of God. The connective action of the object (the mustard seed) and story became a transition point for Christ to engage the listener with the valid message of heart holiness through a life change. The fundamental engagement as a Christ follower is surrendering one's will, judgment, and heart to God. However, for so many, there is a reliance on "other." That is, something other than themselves that they then lack the fortitude to release the worldly ways for God's way.

The "seed" is the ability to reason or relate to what Christ is sharing. If a listener "reasons," they are making rational rather than relational connections with the storyteller, imparting their attributes on the situation, and not trusting God in the process. Christ is in the seed birthed through collaboration with the redeemed person who has accepted Christ into their heart. They must allow it (Christ) to transform their life and world, and there the kingdom spirit is born.

KINGDOM BUILDING OVER LIFE AND DEATH

As Jesus taught through the story of the mustard seed, one must imagine that many questions had to be left unanswered, at least at first. But as Jesus helped those listening to reflect on what he was sharing, the Spirit of God began to engage their spirits in such a way that it challenged them to think spiritually, critically, and reflectively. If the seed had that much power to grow through what in the natural world would be considered small, what could the power of God do in a person's life? What about your own life? There is power through the transformational words found in Scripture that impacts a hearer with not merely words but steps to deepen their faith and challenge the status quo. Many Christians, and maybe even as you've read this book, have found yourself searching because you are in a spiritual rut. It is natural, human in fact, as Christ saw it long ago. Once identified in your life, the challenge is to move up and out of the spiritual rut and embrace the life God has for you. Get up from the discouragement and out from the spiritual hole you find yourself in and capture the unending love of Christ through your daily walk.

The mustard seed is small, yet through faith, something large comes from it. So too, in your own life, whatever is small: Will the interview go well? Will I ever find a spouse? Will I have a career that makes me happy? God is already there ready to help you navigate through the challenges that you face in life. But what is this life if it's just for promotions and not the promoting of Christ to the lost world?

This passage highlights the power of the word of God transformed and parlayed onto what you might be experiencing today as a Christian. Christ is consistently speaking through the work of the Holy Spirit in your life. That brief interaction at the grocery store with a clerk while you are checking out is a seed moment. The coworker who challenges you to meet the deadline on a task.

Or even your child who barely speaks to you as they are lost in their devices as you shuttle them from one activity to the other. It is in the mundane that the Master comes to visit. But too many folks miss him because they are trapped in the mundaneness of life and miss the moments of ministry that he has brought you and through.

Why don't you pause today, reflect, and review your life? What seems like life and death and reflect on it? When you spend time alone with your thoughts you begin to see what seems big is really small, and what is small is growing to be really big as you begin to replace self with a Savior focus.

KINGDOM BUILDING IN THE "NOW"

Every week it seems I am going to McDonald's at least twice a week. I promise it is not for me, really. It is for my son who loves the place. He orders the same thing each time, a cheeseburger Happy Meal, extra fries, and large iced tea. There is one thing, however, he does not like about the meal: the pickles. My son does not care for pickles hot or cold, but I do. In the relationship of now he desires a cheeseburger but does not like everything that comes with it. So invariably he hands me his pickles. I love pickles. He does not realize just yet that the order could be placed without pickles, but I want his pickles.

Here in this passage (Mark 4:30–33) the reader could miss the directional focus of what Christ is sharing if they only focus on the "small seed" and not what Christ could do with the seed. Like the story with my son and pickles, sometimes we get caught up on the "thing" and miss the main message that God is developing something so much better for your life. Serving as a church leader, I am captivated by seed moments in other people's lives. The seed moments are good and bad and take on many forms for the one going through the triumph or struggle.

Think about this: how many times do you think you missed your "seed moment" because you were looking for the "big thing" to happen, and instead, God used the "small seed" to develop something far deeper in your life than instant gratification? Every day, in every way, you have an opportunity to see God in the now. The kingdom of now builds upon the work of spiritual transformation in speaking with the Lord, reading his word, praying, and listening to what the Lord says. The transformative nature of the "now" enhances what is taking place in your daily walk.

Let's give you an exercise of living in the "now" of God. As you drive to work or leave your house today, observe what is happening around you, not just what is before you as you drive. We often get so caught up in what is happening on the road ahead that we miss what God is doing on the edges of our faith through daily interactions. What do you see on the edges of your drive? A person mowing their lawn? An older person walking down the street? It's in these small "now" moments that God gives us a glimpse of an opportunity to learn from and pour into others.

What if you slowed down and waved at the walker or said hello to the neighbor mowing the lawn? Could God use that as a "seed moment" of teaching that could transform your life or the one you are interacting with? I bet it could. The kingdom of God is built on small actions, one relationship at a time. But will you take the time to plant your seed in the kingdom?

HAS GOD'S RULE SPREAD THROUGH YOUR ENTIRE LIFE?

It is almost easy to say that God is the ruler over your life on Sunday morning, but then Tuesday comes, and your child gets in trouble at school, your car breaks down, and your boss calls you out in a meeting in front of your coworkers. Within hours, God reminds you that he is the ruler over all of your life. I get it. It does not sound possible that he cares about your Tuesday problems, but he does. In a series of passages immediately following the one we've focused on, Mark writes about the transformational Jesus in more detail. We see a mighty move of God from Mark 4:35–41 (Jesus calms the storm), Mark 5:1–19 (Jesus restores a demon-possessed man), and Mark 5:21–43 (Jesus raises a dead girl and heals a sick woman); you see how God uses Tuesdays (difficult days and circumstances) to transform believers' lives for the better.

Through these Scriptures, you see a God who rules over the physical world, as seen in Mark 4:35–41; a God who rules over the spiritual world in Mark 5:1–19; and a God who rules over life and death in Mark 5:21–43. In each of these moments, God showed up and provided a seed of faith amid the trial and turmoil of his people. Have you ever thought, "If God could do it for them, why not me?" That's a good question: "Why not you?" Is it because you have not made God ruler over your life? Realize the power that is inside of you as a child of God. God wants to help you. When you stop and think about it, God has demonstrated time and again that he is an all-powerful God who moves in both the physical and spiritual worlds, affecting life and death. God loves you, and because he does, he wants to help in any way possible to transform your life for the better.

You might have asked before, "If God loves me, why do bad things happen to good people?" Again, another good question that shows God cares. We are living in the present reality of God's rule as we wait for its fullness at Jesus' return. Think about this way: "the now, and the not yet." Sound familiar? There will be a day when sin will have no power over your life and those you love. But, until that day, when you are fully healed of the sin nature in your life, you must cling to the seed of faith. That small mustard seed faith will grow over time through prayer, reading the word, and seeking godly counsel in your daily walk. The physical road breaks down as you get older, but God will see you through. The spiritual road is not easy, but it is made easier with God when you fully surrender and commit your life to him. As you come to the end of your life, you see with fresh eyes the value found in life and death, for God is the way-maker. And there it is again, the now and the not yet.

CONCLUDING PRAYER CHALLENGE

As God moves in the details of your life, take some time to reflect on how God is speaking to you. This might mean disconnecting from your devices, taking out a pen and paper, and writing down what God is saying. Alternatively, you could take a walk alone and allow your mind to wander, clearing out all the thoughts that come to mind. You will find in the still silence of that walk, after all the worries are cleared, that God begins to speak into your life. Many times, you might find yourself searching for a "*big* sign" when God speaks through the "small mustard seed" of faith.

As you end this chapter, why not pause and pray for mustard seed faith? "Lord, in the season of the now and not yet, I wait on you. You know my faith, my story, and what I am going through. What I need now more than ever is your wisdom to overcome by focusing not on the problem, but on you, the problem-solver. Please help me to see the unseen, as I rely on your guidance to strengthen and grow my faith. I cling to my mustard seed faith as I wait in the now and not yet. In Jesus' name, amen."

7

The Seed of the Imperishable

Living in the Imperishable Word of God Through Which We Are Born Again

TWENTY YEARS AGO, I walked into a small church in an urban neighborhood of Hialeah, Florida, where a prayer and fasting meeting was to take place. Many of the participants represented diverse ethnicities, and several different languages were spoken, but they were all part of the same holiness denomination. Glancing around, I realized that the sights and sounds of the meeting to come would provide a small glimpse of what heaven must be like, but I was not there for a cultural lesson, but was on a search for who God wanted me to be. I felt a tugging, maybe even a longing, in my heart for something more. That was a deeper relationship with Jesus.

Deep within my spirit, the day I was born, God had planted an imperishable seed that had taken root. Darkened by worldly sin, hidden from the fruits of what would come, there it lay dormant for decades, waiting for me to accept the calling on my life. Ministry, as they say, is not just a mere vocation; it is a calling that transforms a normal life into something God-honoring. That imperishable seed is not just planted in me, but it's in you. Deep within the recesses of your spirit is a calling that is longing to grow and become a manifestation of what God is leading you to.

THE IMPERISHABLE NATURE OF THE GOSPEL EMPOWERS US TO OVERCOME THE FEAR OF LOVING OTHERS AND TO BE INITIATORS OF LASTING, UNCONDITIONAL LOVE

1 PETER 1:22–25

22 Now that you have purified yourselves by obeying the truth so that you have sincere love for each other, love one another deeply, from the heart. 23 For you have been born again, not of perishable seed, but of imperishable, through the living and enduring word of God. 24 For, "All people are like grass and all their glory is like the flowers of the field; the grass withers and the flowers fall, 25 but the word of the Lord endures forever." And this is the word that was preached to you.

There it is. Did you catch it? The "imperishable, through the living and enduring word of God." The imperishable seed is not our own, but it is God's. Inside of you, the seed he planted, he waters, and he is bringing to light is not yours, but his. Consider that God allows you to be a part of what he is trying to accomplish in your life and in the lives of those you interact with. For me, it was understanding this that led me to be willing to lay down everything at that altar decades ago. What about you? What are you holding on to that God is asking you to give up? Family, work, finances, and so on? Do not let today slip by without leaving it at the foot of the cross.

WE HAVE BORN AGAIN IN THE LIVING HOPE

Peter had a long and storied history with Jesus. Simon (Peter's name before Jesus changed it) was serving his family and building a little fishing charter business with his brother and co-owner Andrew when the Lord came by and called both of them to be "fishers of men" (Matt 4:18–22). In that one moment, the perishable became imperishable. Jesus radically changed Peter's life for the better. Inside of you is the imperishable seed that is being called, much like Peter, to step out and into your destiny. Sure, it's nerve-racking and unsettling, but you may have become so accustomed to worldly ways that it's become comfortable, and God is calling you to change your name. In the new name, you will receive new hope as you are born again.

That hope is not found in the known worldly experiences, but in the unknown, when you rely on God to be your guide in your daily walk. It's in the pattern of faith that your Father reveals his plan for your life and ministry and radically changes your life. Hope is not something dreamed of, but found when you fully commit to Christ.

WE ARE CALLED TO LIVE OUR FAITH IN HOLINESS AS EXILES

As Peter continued to walk with Christ, he began learning the advantages of being a follower. People would call to him and ask him to heal or help them, but he was not fully committed to what it took to be a follower of the Way. Jesus made it look easy, but as pressure began to mount on the disciples, Peter reacted not in a Christlike way, but through anger and vitriol. The pain of the world reared its head when Peter lashed out in anger with a sword and cut the right ear off of a Roman soldier who was doing his job, arresting Jesus (John 18:10–15). Jesus' example in that moment is one that, later, as Peter reflected, would help him through his exile living under oppression.

Maybe your faith has been shaken by what has happened to you or around you. It's human nature to want to lash out and strike back at the person or situation that has brought you so much pain. But it is in the promises found in the imperishable seed that your Spirit is reminded that God is doing a new work in you. Just because you feel like you are living in exile does not mean you have to act like it. The truth is that God has a breakout plan for your life if you will cling to his hope.

WE ARE BEING BUILT INTO A SPIRITUAL HOUSE

Poor Peter, he could not catch a break. Sound familiar? He began to struggle with guilt over his outburst; perhaps he felt ashamed that he had allowed his anger to get in the way of his judgment. He wanted to help Jesus, but his flesh kept him from walking in faith. There is an honesty that comes through this truth. It is a reminder that whatever you are facing, whatever you have done, Christ can lead you through it. In Luke 22:54–62, we begin to see more deeply the exile that Peter is walking into. In a single night, he will deny Jesus three times. Locking eyes with Jesus, he knew at that moment he was a big disappointment.

From walking with Jesus to denying him within hours, Peter entered exile relatively quickly. Do you see yourself in Peter, desiring to be more closely aligned with Christ, yet finding yourself further from him? But what did Christ and Peter do in this moment? Christ went forward to the cross for Peter, and Peter left, regretful and crying. Exile is painful. Exile punishes, but it prepares the believer for what is to come. What was coming was faith in holiness.

After Jesus' death on the cross and resurrection, something healing took place that instilled in Peter a new faith and hope for the season he had entered. It would sustain him until his earthly death, from prison bars to a passion for sharing about Christ. Through a simple but robust conversation with Jesus (John 21:15–19), Peter found hope, love, and forgiveness all in a series of questions from Jesus.

WE DO NOT FEAR THE UNKNOWN AS TEMPORARY OR EVEN CONDITIONAL

Philophobia is the fear of love or being loved. "Philo" means "love," and "phobia" means "fear"—sounds like Peter. Well, let me explain. Peter loved Jesus, but within hours of Jesus' arrest, Peter was seized with fear that he too would be swept up and arrested. Peter's friends were all hiding, but Peter wanted to see his teacher and try to help. In John 18:15–18, the reader sees Peter following, yearning to be with Jesus, but is frightened by the world around him. Who can he trust? Who can he ask for help? Watching from a distance, in the shadows, Peter finds himself with a choice: to let others know he is a follower or to reject the one he followed.

In that moment, a choice arose—a very human one, I believe. Perhaps you have also faced it: choosing Jesus or turning to worldly pursuits. When Peter rejected Jesus, the fire raged to keep the onlookers warm. As Peter rejected Jesus the fire raged to keep the onlookers warm; the fire of the world overtook Peter's selfish nature as he denied Christ in front of the small group for a second time. There it was, Peter fearing love. If he had fully expressed his love for Christ, he too most likely would have been arrested, he must have felt. In his mind, Peter could not take that chance.

WE FEAR BECAUSE WE BELIEVE WE'RE NOT GOOD ENOUGH

Peter realized he was not like his teacher; he could not stand up to the powers that be and challenge the status quo. He thought he could, but here in the cold darkness surrounded by the warmth of a fire, he rejects his colleague; more than that, he rejects his mentor. The spirit of shame must have passed through him in that moment. Self-doubt and talk began to sink in; here for the second time he rejects Christ. The pain he felt during that hour is felt by many of us in our walk when we come up short. Ask yourself: how do I reject the world and not Christ?

Inside you, as it was Peter that night, is the gift of imperishable seed that cannot be snuffed out by the darkness of sin, or even in the light of hell's flames; only you can give it away by rejecting the Lord. That is what Peter did. But watch what happens: God does something new, even though rejection has taken place.

THE IMPERISHABLE SEED BURIED BUT NOT DEAD

Matthew's Gospel recounts Peter's denial story in quick succession (Matt 26:60–70, 71–72, 73–74). All four Gospels share highlights of what happened that night. Have you ever stopped and wondered why? It may be that Jesus knows you and understands the human nature you were born into. Perhaps he wanted you to see firsthand one he walked with, taught, and loved in the end rejected him. All too human, yet in the humanness of life, Christ's love extended to Peter and could extend to you even now.

Let's pause and go back to the beginning. Not of this chapter, but of your life, long before you came to know the Lord. In Genesis, the opening words of Scripture read, "In the beginning God created the heavens and the earth" (Gen 1:1). In that moment, he was thinking of you. Let that sink in. As he formed the world, he was creating the seed that he would place inside of you—one that was perishable in worldly ways, but one that could not die in faith. If the story of Peter were the world's story, it would have ended in rejection of faith, fellowship, and a further walk with God. But Peter's story is about the imperishable seed, a faith rejuvenated through Christ's love and forgiveness. That promise, that healing in the forgiveness is for you, dear reader. John 21:15 restores the lost, broken, and disheartened sea of humanity through the example of Peter and Jesus' relationship.

John 21:15

When they had finished eating, Jesus said to Simon Peter, "Simon, son of John, do you love me more than these?" "Yes, Lord," he said, "you know that I love you." Jesus said, "Feed my lambs."

In this brief conversation, Christ restores Peter and sets him on a new path, presenting a new challenge: "Feed my lambs." From rejection to restoration, Peter is transformed to begin again. What was that? It was the imperishable seed taking root and starting to grow in favor of the Lord. Life might have challenged you through rejection. Maybe you lost your job, found yourself on the wrong side of an argument, and could not figure out how to patch a relationship with a dear friend, or failed to get the promotion you were counting on. All of these were perishable days. Days when you lost what you had longed for. In times like these, when it seems the whole world is retreating from you, God moves toward you. He embraces you. Like Peter, he sees the imperishable seed he has planted in you. It inspires him; it challenges him to help you restore what has been lost.

Do not allow the adversary to convince you that you are not good enough. When the Lord looks at you, he sees "more than enough." He sees an overcomer, a called warrior, a gifted leader, and an anointed soul. From rejection to restoration, he is moving in your favor. Like Peter before, he forgives the former things and sees what you are stepping into, the future you. Peter would go on to win many souls to the Lord. Preaching the gospel in small and large groups, from towns to cities, he shared the gospel unashamedly. He had learned from his past and stood in the presence of the Lord even when he was being persecuted for his faith and belief system. He moved from rejecting Christ to being restored by him.

Whatever you have faced in your journey is nothing compared to what God has in store for you in the future. He is getting ready to turn your pain into your gain by moving you from rejection to restoration. I cannot help but think back nearly two decades to how I felt as I walked out of the church. For the first time, I felt free, as if a veil had been lifted that had been covering my eyes, and I could see more clearly.

Within hours, my new faith was challenged as I shared with my wife that I had been called; she said, "Called to what?" When I told her that I had been called into ministry, she was surprised, to say the least. When I shared the same thoughts with a pastor, he challenged me and said, "I don't think you are called into ministry." Both of these people loved me, but they did not see the imperishable seed planted deep within me. How could they? I just learned it was there myself. Over time, they have become my biggest supporters and cheerleaders as they saw the seed of faith take root more publicly.

Right now, there are people in your life who are planting their seeds of doubt, frustration, and pain into your life. They are projecting their value onto you. But know this truth: their values matter to them, but not to you. You are the one called. You are the one planted with the seed of imperishable faith. Do not let anyone take that from you, for you have moved from rejection to restoration in Christ's eyes. Like Peter before you, you have learned a new lesson and realized the power of the seed of faith planted within you. Challenge yourself to let it grow by watering it daily through prayer, the reading of God's word, and obeying his will for your life.

CONCLUDING PRAYER CHALLENGE

Peter must have realized on the third rejection that he was rejecting Christ and rejecting his future. Maybe you have seen yourself in the story of Peter. By accepting the word of God for himself, he changed from the inside out. For years, he had head knowledge, but now Peter had heart knowledge. How about you? You may have been the smartest person in the room. Success has come easily, but then you hit a roadblock. Instead of continuing to reject Christ, allow him to restore you. Peter's story provides a new way forward. He teaches three major points that you might reflect on:

1. **Love costs something.** Rejecting the world could cost what you cherish the most.
2. **There is no promise without pain.** You must surrender worldly desires to step up and receive what God has in store for you.
3. **The seed in you must grow.** Water God's seed by reading the word of God daily, praying daily, and seeking fellowship with other believers.

As you end this chapter, why not pause and pray for the imperishable seed to grow inside of you?

Father, you have planted deep inside of me a seed that no man could extinguish, so Lord, fan into flame a fire that burns inside of me to overtake my sinful nature, so that I might reject the world, while I resonate in your spirit daily. Please help me, like Peter, to see my faults and, instead of falling into self-pity, seek your face in forgiveness. Encourage me to believe again in the restorative power that comes from calling out your name.

Like Peter before, forgive me of my sins, and help me to love you and your people more, in Jesus' mighty name, amen.

8

The Seed of a Harvest of Righteousness

Reaping the Harvest to Come

WALKING THROUGH THE CHURCH doors, it felt, in some ways, as if I were stepping back in time. The foyer was not much bigger than a master bedroom walk-in closet of a new house on the market today. However, it lacked anything modern. Wood-paneled walls darkened the entranceway, and even the fluorescent light above seemed dim. On the walls were plaques and pictures, along with a trophy case that held awards from a bygone era. Literature was placed under a well-worn bulletin board that had once held events but had not been removed. An umbrella stand with a sorted umbrella and jackets hung above it looked as if the entryway were someone's home and not God's house.

Stepping through the double doors that led from the foyer into the sanctuary, a number board was placed proudly to the left of the platform, and to its right was a hymn board that recounted the hymns to be sung. Behind the podium, a large picture of Jesus was displayed, knocking and seeking after the congregation. The pews were lightly filled with not more than two dozen people spread out in a sanctuary that could seat over one hundred. The question being asked was: "Where is the harvest?" While the pastor and the remaining members did not ask it that way, that is what they meant. These individuals had been faithful in many ways, yet their faithfulness did not receive reciprocation from the community. Where was their harvest?

In spending time with dying churches as a church revitalization strategist, I, too, have asked, "God, where is the harvest?" There is an emptiness when you realize, somewhere along the way, that a church must have gone wrong or ignored its prompting, which led to decline. So, maybe you're not in a dying church, but how is your faith? Without faith, the church will die, but more importantly, you will die. Your spiritual health is far greater than a building or church campus. If denominations will spend millions of dollars to keep the dying church alive, what do you think God would pay to save you?

God paid it forward to save you through the life, death, and resurrection of Jesus Christ. What a priceless gift! Yet, for many, they await another harvest of "things" and not souls of loved ones and current unbelievers.

THE CHURCH IS THE FIELD IN WHICH GOD SOWS HIS WORD AND AUTHORITY TO REAP A HARVEST OF RIGHTEOUSNESS

1 CORINTHIANS 3:5–9

5 What, after all, is Apollos? And what is Paul? Only servants, through
whom you came to believe—as the Lord has assigned to each his task.
6 I planted the seed, Apollos watered it, but God has been making it
grow. 7 So neither the one who plants nor the one who waters is anything, but only God, who makes things grow. 8 The one who plants and
the one who waters have one purpose, and they will each be rewarded
according to their own labor. 9 For we are co-workers in God's service;
you are God's field, God's building.

WHO ARE YOU CALLED TO BE

Everyone in the church, you included, is called to serve in some capacity. It is clear from this passage of Scripture that the harvest of righteousness is not built on one person, but built on a team of people working together to lift others who are struggling. Reread the Scripture above so you become more familiar with it. After you do, go back and underline where Paul writes in this epistle that describes Christian leadership. Do you see it? If not, let me help. Here are seven leadership traits on servanthood that I found:

1. Servants through whom people come to believe. (v. 5)
2. Servants to whom the Lord assigns those who come to believe. (v. 5)
3. Servants who are planters and servants who are waterers. (v. 6)
4. Servants should not take credit for themselves. (v. 7)
5. Servants are to serve others, not just the local church. (v. 7)
6. Servants who serve the Lord are the ones who receive wages. (v. 8)
7. Servants are God's fellow workers. (v. 9)

Do you see it? You are called to serve. In fact, God is calling you to help the church move forward. Many Sundays, you might have felt, "Do I have to go?" and the simple answer is, yes. God has a perfect plan for your life and ministry, and he is calling you to draw closer to him. These seven characteristics of Christian leadership highlight the path and direction that servants are called to follow. However, in many churches, the struggle is not with people, but with getting them to hear the call of God to move from the pew into partnership with others in their neighborhood, workplace, or community. God is speaking of the harvest, but it begins with a harvester who is ready to serve.

Pause for a moment and reflect on that and ask yourself: Am I serving where God wants me to serve? Serving is not just attending. Serving involves actively participating in the life of the church, such as teaching Sunday school, assisting in the office, and cleaning the church. Servanthood is giving oneself over to the local church for God to use, then going into the mission field to win souls for Jesus. It begins as a humble servant and ends as a harvester of souls. Does that sound like you?

WHO ARE YOU REALLY

Far too many churches have few too many people serving in any capacity within the church walls. Have you ever wondered, "Why has God not brought more people in?" Could it be that the people who are currently in the church could do what needs to be done, but they are not as faithful? Now, I am not talking about you, but the majority of churches are struggling with this fundamental issue of servanthood. Two types of people make up the church found in verse 9; let's look at it again with fresh eyes.

1 CORINTHIANS 3:9

For we are co-workers in God's service; you are God's field, God's building.

God's field and God's building stand out in this verse. Where do you fit in when it comes to God's service in the church? In the field or building? When one looks at the work in the field, one sees opportunities to share Christ with others rather liberally. Throughout your day, people are brought across your path who will either challenge, hinder, or excite you by sharing with them. Some of these interactions are mundane tasks, such as saying "Good morning" to a coworker or placing an order at a local fast-food restaurant for breakfast, but it's in the margins of the mundane that God works, if you will allow him. When you begin to see the field as an opportunity, rather than just a regular part of life, you start to capture the imagination of what God could do through you—and thus through the local church.

WHAT IS THE CHURCH REALLY FOR?

Your local church was not planted by accident, but by divine appointment when he led planters to that very site it sits on today. What a legacy you get to be a part of serving in this hallowed space. Even your leadership, and drawing to the church, was God-divine for the season you are in. The church needs you, and you need the church. It has been said, "The church is not a building; it's the people." Why, yes, but the building is a tool, an instrument of God's people in the community where it was planted. For many legacy churches, the "tool" has received tourniquet after tourniquet to patch it together but never fixing the real problems. If the church wants a harvest, it must work the field with the tools they already have.

Much like in your spiritual life, church can be a one-day, one-hour-a-week tourniquet for your spiritual life, but it does not heal you because you have failed to fully surrender your life to the Lord, read his word daily, pray, and seek his counsel. The Great Physician, our Lord, loves you more than you realize. He has a fantastic plan not only for you but for the church property. What if you, as a leader, looked at the church campus through the eyes of Christ? What is underutilized? What needs fixing? What can be moved to open up a new opportunity to connect with a community group or partner? It sounds so simple, yet many churches and their leaders are failing to see the harvest of righteousness that could be had through an investment in the campus to reconnect to the community.

You have immense potential within you and in your service to the local church. If you focus on the God field in front of you and the God building where you gather weekly, he will help you reach your full potential as you help others.

THE HARVEST TO COME

The church members waited. They waited for the right pastor. They waited for a family with children to attend. They waited for more funds to be included in the offering plate. They waited for the neighborhood to embrace them. They waited. In the end the church lost the waiting game. Waiting slowly killed their calling, drive, and prayer life. Waiting led to discouragement, frustration, and a sense of giving up. God did not call you nor the church to wait. So, here I was, walking into the church that was struggling, and they were waiting for me to share something so profound that it would radically grow the church.

What I shared was 1 Cor 3:5–9, and the servant leadership principles that came from this passage. Like a lead balloon, the people became deflated. They wanted a silver bullet program, person, or partnership, and instead, I brought them Jesus. Why Jesus? Because Jesus is the only answer to reaping a harvest of righteousness. You cannot spiritually fake your way through a genuine relationship with Jesus. You must do the hard work of reflecting, praying, seeking forgiveness, and accepting it to be truly rooted and ready for the harvest work that is to come.

THE FOCUS SHOULD BE ON JESUS, NOT THE PASTOR

There is a tendency in the local church that when things begin to turn around and God seems to be on the move, members start to celebrate their pastor by putting the pastor above others. While pastors appreciate support and encouragement, they are not the end-all be-all when it comes to the local church. Pastors are called leaders, not local celebrities or all-knowing individuals who are without fault. Ask the spouse of a pastor, including mine, and they will give you an earful. The reality is, pastors are like you; they are called to serve. Servanthood is not attached to a title, but it is connected to serving others to win the harvest of souls for the kingdom.

Jesus should be the focus. Let me change that to say, Jesus is the focus. Jesus is the focus of all projects, programs, and partnerships formed within and outside the local church. By placing less emphasis on a pastor and more emphasis on Jesus, you begin to see Jesus everywhere and desire more and more to win the harvest (lost souls) for Jesus.

THE FOCUS SHOULD BE ON EMPHASIZING PEOPLE OF GOD COLLECTIVELY THAN SELF

It seems every church and every member wants a harvest from God, but the question one must ask is, "Am I willing to do my part?" In the church that was dying, mentioned several times in this chapter, they had to believe deep down inside what they were saying out loud: "We want to live." They had to do their part in building the kingdom of God around them. Much like this church, you have a calling, maybe even an obligation, placed on your life by God to invest in others. In John 4:35, it reminds the reader that the harvest field is "white," meaning it is ready for you and the local church to do their part in winning souls. The key set of words in the previous sentence is "do your part." Serving God is easy when you act on what Scripture challenges you to obey. The hard part comes when you disobey God yet still desire the treasure of the harvest.

The work of a harvester is not to be done alone. It must be fulfilled collectively by working together with others to share the gospel, by telling your story, and inviting others into a relationship with the Lord. Realize it is not just bringing them to church; it is more than that. It is establishing a relationship that helps them gain a relationship with Christ. Collectively, this is done in your personal life with those you are comfortable talking with. It's done in your professional life with coworkers and bosses that you interact with. When done in the Spirit of God, a harvest is rendered. Perhaps not at first, but over time, as the relationship deepens and the Lord guides.

THE FOCUS SHOULD BE ON WINNING SOULS AND RESTORING YOUR OWN RELATIONSHIP WITH GOD

As a follower of Christ, your role should be to remove the restrictions of your affections, thoughts, and processes to reach where God wants you to go. This is challenging for many because it involves giving up a part of yourself and surrendering to Christ. For many, perhaps even for you, you've come to a place where you feel you've given God most of your things. You are faithful in tithing, volunteering in the church, and serving where needed, but you realize it's not enough. You may even feel uncertain about what to do next. You want to see a harvest, but something is holding you back. Let me be honest, I get it. I do.

So, if the focus is on souls, how can you win someone to the Lord? A simple way is to look for friends (neighbors, coworkers, even social media connections) and reach out to them to meet up. The only agenda is fellowship, and before you are done with that meal, coffee, or gathering, set the next date to meet again. Over time, begin to share your journey not only of life, but of your spiritual life. Realize you are not using a program to win someone; you are sharing your heart. Throughout these faith-sharing moments, ask God to speak to the other person's heart and to be open to the gospel message. Let me pause again to point something out you might have missed. If you only have Christian friends, then consider expanding your friend group or at least your social circle so you can be the harvest collector you desire to be.

In the end, these "spirit times" will be great socially and provide you with a soft-evangelism approach to sharing your faith in a nonthreatening way.

CONCLUDING PRAYER CHALLENGE

The harvesters of righteousness sees the need around them and moves toward it over time. In a research study produced by Barna, titled "The Great Disconnect," it challenges the church (you included) to see the community around you as a mission field that is ripe for harvest. Let's close this chapter by focusing on four key missional reconnects that you can work on.

Reconnect by Meeting Spiritual and Physical Needs

Realize that each day you have an opportunity to share your faith with someone that you come across. Begin to pray each morning as you wake up that God will bring you the right person and the proper conversation to share what God can do for them in their lives. This requires a spiritual presence, but also a physical one that connects the self to the Savior.

Increase Your Biblical Literacy

This will take intentionality in your life to download a Bible app on your phone and click on a daily Bible reading plan, or getting out your Bible and reading a chapter a day and then reflecting on what the Lord is speaking to you by writing it down in a journal. Biblical literacy is not just listening to the pastor on Sunday or even studying for a sermon if you are a pastor; it is surrendering your time over to God to learn and grow through his word.

Realize That the Center of Christianity Has Shifted

The church is far larger and greater than your spirit or even the local church. For many denominations, there are thousands of churches and millions of members connected to a larger calling. That calling has shifted from the United States to other parts of the world as the gospel continues to expand and spread far beyond the shores of the United States. While it is exciting to see the gospel spread, it challenges us in the North American church to reconnect to Christ and to serve more faithfully at home in winning a local harvest.

Increase the Level of Transparency and Trustworthiness

Turn on the television, read a blog, or view your social media app, and you'll find out rather quickly that trust and transparency have failed when it comes to viewing leadership. The erosion of trust and transparency has eroded the respect and belief in the pastor-member relationship within the church. When speaking to a non-Christian, it gets even worse. To rebuild trust and win the harvest, you have to be intentional about developing long-term relationships. Relationships build trust, which in turn creates opportunities to share more about Jesus.

In the end, every step toward the harvest of righteousness should be bathed in prayer, promoted by the Holy Spirit, and surrendered over to God.

Epilogue

The Challenge Ahead

At the outset of our time together, the first chapter mentioned living in proximity to local apple orchards famous for their many indulgent treats. Though not diet-friendly, it is a great place to venture onto side roads and trails for moments of prayerful meditation and time with the Lord. The many old sheds and farming equipment facilitate prayers, all reminding us of the decades of sowing and reaping. There are times of sowing, waiting, and reaping. Will you wait? As you consider the words of this book, we encourage you to get alone with the Father.

As you venture into these spaces of reflective prayer, consider our initial analogy. Remember, it is not how many apples you have in your cart, but more importantly, how many seeds are in the apples. The seeds we have discussed reside within God's people as they grow in Christlikeness. Planting and watering these seeds is our task as Christian leaders and pastors. They will produce a harvest within their heart that generates and transfers life and growth in others. Remain the patient farmer sowing seeds. Stop counting apples and begin focusing on the seeds within.

To accomplish this, a significant and targeted shift in your prayer life may be necessary. Like many leaders, you are overwhelmed with immediate needs. Matters concerning staff, volunteers, facilities, and finances become all-consuming. Calendars packed with projects and meetings keep us running at a breakneck speed. All these are essential aspects of our ministry efforts, but they can, if not kept in proper order, lead us to act as though we can harvest without planting and watering. Is that a characteristic of your leadership? If so, let's make a change.

As you read the eight preceding chapters, we pray that you have felt a nudge from God to move in a new direction in your walk. Far too many, maybe even you included, have allowed circumstances to become their excuse for not growing in faith. Our challenge to you is not to stop at the eight chapters. But spend the next eight weeks continuing to focus on the Prayer Challenges through reflection, journaling, and prayerful consideration of the chapters you have read.

At the end of the eight weeks ahead, let us challenge you once more to celebrate with a special dinner, speak to a friend about the journey you have been on, or go out for a walk in nature and get alone with God and thank him for how he has reopened your eyes and heart for the next stage of your leadership and ministry. God will use this time through this resource, studying his word, and prayerfully considering what you have thought and acted upon to help guide your spiritual growth in the future.

Trust us when we say, the best days are yet ahead!

Praying for Seeds

Prayer Grid

Seed	Scripture	Prayer
Righteousness	Jer 4:3–4; Hos 10:12	Lord, cleanse our hearts in preparation for your work.
The word of God	Matt 13:1–23 Parable of the Sower	Lord, root your word in the hearts of those who hear.
Our faith	Matt 17:14–21 Faith of a mustard seed	Lord, grow our faith to move the challenges we face in ministry and life.
Trusting the work of the Holy Spirit	Mark 4:26–29 The Parable of the Seed Growing	Lord, help us trust you with the results of our ministry efforts.
The kingdom of God	Mark 4:30–33 The Parable of the Mustard Seed	Lord, grow your kingdom through our ministry.
Living in the word of God through which we are born again	1 Pet 1:22–25 Born of imperishable seed	Lord, help us live out your word that others may be born again.

Eight-Week Journal

Leadership That Generates Spiritual Life and Growth

WEEK 1: THE GENERATION AND TRANSFER OF LIFE AND GROWTH

Scripture: Galatians 1:1–22

What is God saying to you through this passage of Scripture?

____

____

____

____

____

____

How can you use this Scripture to impact others through your understanding of what he is saying to you?

____

____

____

____

____

____

Prayer Challenge: Lord, what ways are my prayers out of line with your word and the calling you placed on my life?

Personal Prayer and Reflection:

WEEK 2: SEEDS THAT PRODUCE A HARVEST OF RIGHTEOUSNESS

Scripture: Jeremiah 4:1–31

What is God saying to you through this passage of Scripture?

How can you use this Scripture to impact others through your understanding of what he is saying to you?

Prayer Challenge: Ask the Holy Spirit to search your heart to seek those you may need to repent to or about due to a challenging situation that has happened.

Personal Prayer and Reflection:

WEEK 3: THE SEED OF THE WORD OF GOD

Scripture: Matthew 13:1–30
What is God saying to you through this passage of Scripture?

How can you use this Scripture to impact others through your understanding of what he is saying to you?

Prayer Challenge: What do you have to do differently that will help others hear, understand, and live out the messages from Sunday service each week?

Personal Prayer and Reflection:

WEEK 4: THE SEED OF FAITH

Scripture: Matthew 17:14–21

What is God saying to you through this passage of Scripture?

How can you use this Scripture to impact others through your understanding of what he is saying to you?

Prayer Challenge: Everyone struggles with unbelief in their faith journey. If you are struggling today, how can God help you with your unbelief to walk in faith and not by fear?

____

____

____

____

____

____

Personal Prayer and Reflection:

____

____

____

____

____

____

WEEK 5: THE SEED OF THE UNSEEN WORK OF THE HOLY SPIRIT

Scripture: Mark 4:26–29

What is God saying to you through this passage of Scripture?

____

____

____

____

____

____

How can you use this Scripture to impact others through your understanding of what he is saying to you?

____

____

____

____

____

Prayer Challenge: Who is God calling you to walk alongside on a spiritual journey of renewal? How will you touch base and encourage them with God's word in the future?

Personal Prayer and Reflection:

WEEK 6: THE SEED OF THE KINGDOM OF GOD

Scripture: Mark 4:30–33

What is God saying to you through this passage of Scripture?

How can you use this Scripture to impact others through your understanding of what he is saying to you?

Prayer Challenge: How is your faith? Is there a mustard seed that you need to put in God's hands to grow? If so, how can God help?

Personal Prayer and Reflection:

WEEK 7: THE SEED OF THE IMPERISHABLE

Scripture: 1 Peter 1:22–25

What is God saying to you through this passage of Scripture?

How can you use this Scripture to impact others through your understanding of what he is saying to you?

Prayer Challenge: How can the imperishable seed grow inside of you and be used to advance the kingdom in others?

Personal Prayer and Reflection:

WEEK 8: THE SEED OF A HARVEST OF RIGHTEOUSNESS

Scripture: 1 Corinthians 3:5–9

What is God saying to you through this passage of Scripture?

How can you use this Scripture to impact others through your understanding of what he is saying to you?

Prayer Challenge: Who in your sphere of influence needs a relationship with Jesus Christ? What steps can you do to help them better understand what it means to have that relationship?

Personal Prayer and Reflection:

Other Books by the Authors

BY DESMOND BARRETT

Addition Through Subtraction: Revitalizing the Established Church. Eugene, OR: Wipf & Stock, 2022.

Confidence for Leadership: Power Strategies for the Established Church. Coauthored with David M. Church and Paul T. Hobbs. Eugene, OR: Wipf & Stock, 2023.

Helping the Small Church Win Guests: Preparing to Increase Attendance. Eugene, OR: Wipf & Stock, 2024.

Missional Reset: Capturing the Heart for Local Missions in the Established Church. Coauthored with Charlotte P. Holter. Eugene, OR: Wipf & Stock, 2023.

Revitalize to Plant: Reshaping the Established Church to Plant Churches. Coauthored with Dr. Jeffery D. Skinner. Eugene, OR: Wipf and Stock, 2023.

Revitalizing the Declining Church: From Death's Door to Community Growth. Eugene, OR: Wipf & Stock, 2021.

Rising from the Ashes into Church Renewal. Eugene, OR: Wipf & Stock, 2025.

BY PAUL T. HOBBS

Confidence for Leadership: Power Strategies for the Established Church. Coauthored with David M. Church and Paul T. Hobbs. Eugene, OR: Wipf & Stock, 2023.

About the Authors

Dr. Desmond Barrett is the lead pastor at Hilltop Church (Detroit First Church of the Nazarene) in metro-Detroit. He is the author of multiple books and the host of the podcast Revitalizing the Declining Church with Dr. Desmond Barrett. Dr. Barrett has conducted extensive research on church revitalization and serves as a church revitalizer, consultant, coach, and mentor to revitalizing pastors and churches.

He is a graduate of Nazarene Bible College (Bachelor of Ministry) and Trevecca Nazarene University (Master of Organizational Leadership, and Doctor of Education in Leadership and Professional Practice).

Dr. Paul T. Hobbs is the lead pastor of The Retreat Church in Yucaipa, California. He trains pastors and mentors those working towards ordination in the Church of the Nazarene. In addition to his work with pastors, he spent 17 years teaching secondary Bible and Theology classes for two Christian High Schools.

He is a graduate of Nazarene Bible College (Bachelor of Biblical Studies), Liberty Baptist Theological Seminary (Master of Arts in Religion with a focus on Leadership), and Grand Canyon University (Doctorate of Education in Organizational Leadership and Christian Ministry).

www.ingramcontent.com/pod-product-compliance
Lightning Source LLC
LaVergne TN
LVHW020650100826
845148LV00012B/2416

* 9 7 9 8 3 8 5 2 7 1 2 6 9 *